GAUGAMELA
Hard-won victory
over the second
Persian army.
Darius flees to
high Iran

DAMGHAN

Darius is abandoned by
his remaining supporters
and found dying by
a Macedonian soldier

← The Caspian Gates

ECBATANA

New base for the
eastern campaign,
commanded by Parmenion,
later murdered here.

Euphrates

Tigris

BABYLON
323 BC

Order restored and
preparations made for
an expedition to Arabia,
the Red Sea and Ethiopia.
Alexander succumbs to an
attack of fever

SUSA

330 BC

324 BC

The Persian Gates →

PERSEPOLIS
Vast quantities of booty
seized and palaces partly
burned down

ALEXANDER THE GREAT

Power as Destiny

ALEXANDER

PETER BAMM

THE GREAT

Power as Destiny

256 illustrations, 16 color plates

Translated from the German by J. Maxwell Brownjohn

McGraw-Hill Book Company · New York

EDITORIAL AND RESEARCH: Ronald Davidson-Houston BA, FRAI

Ann G. Ward ph D, BA

LAYOUT: Pauline Baines MSIA

© 1968 Droemersche Verlagsanstalt AG Zurich and Thames and Hudson Ltd
London
Library of Congress Catalog Card Number 68–26310

Text film-set in England by Keyspools Ltd Golborne Lancashire

Printed & bound in West Germany by Mohndruck Reinhard Mohn OHG Gutersloh

03596

CONTENTS

Alexander in battle, mounted on Bucephalus. Bronze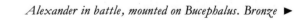

TO BE DESTINED FOR POWER is a divine gift from Pandora's Box. To inherit power has always been an advantage. Although legitimacy does not remove the need to commit the acts of violence entailed by the possession of power, inheritance may at least preclude the crimes which attend its acquisition. All ancient civilizations hailed the charisma of legitimacy. Even when it was only one generation old, inherited power was regarded as legitimate power, and its aura did not fade until the French Revolution. Napoleon's obeisance to the apostolic house of Habsburg was no more than a cynical gesture on the part of a latter-day usurper.

The power which Alexander inherited from Philip, his father, was legitimate; that which he acquired by conquest was not. Subsequently, as successor to the Achaemenids, the Macedonian king practised a great deal of toleration and shrewd restraint in an attempt to invest his sovereignty over Persia with the character of legitimacy. Having completed his conquest of the Persian Empire, he married Princess Stateira, eldest daughter of Darius III, the last king of Persia. Any son of this marriage would have been born with a legitimate claim to the whole empire, but the marriage remained without issue. Roxana, Alexander's first wife and a daughter of Oxyartes, a petty king from the Karakorum, engineered the luckless Stateira's murder after they had both been widowed. Her motive for this crime was a wish to secure exclusive legitimacy for the son whom she had borne shortly after Alexander's death. When, years later, Cassander had Roxana and her son Alexander murdered in their turn, his object was nothing more nor less than the destruction of that legitimacy. The young Alexander's death spelt the final extinction of the Argeads, the royal line from which Alexander the Great traced his descent.

9

Power should act, not talk, as Goethe says in *Maximen und Reflexionen*. Our information about the motives of men who make world history may be scanty, but there is one motive common to all. Like lesser mortals, men in authority have always felt the need to place their actions on a moral basis. The possession of power had to be legitimate, but, more than that, the wielding of it had to accord with the will of the gods. This was regarded as a moral obligation from the time of Socrates onwards, and the exchange of letters between Alexander and Darius after the battle of Issus provides a striking illustration of just how seriously this obligation was taken.

Some political dealings are inherently just; others, for all their supreme expediency, are supremely unjust. It is the latter which stand in greatest need of moral camouflage. Truth and hypocrisy both acknowledge justice to be the overriding principle which ought to govern all action.

Socrates would no doubt have rubbed his bulbous nose with satisfaction had it been granted to him to see how conscience began to impinge on world history. Equally, he would not have been too surprised to note that, as just dealing diminishes with the growth of power, so the cogency of moral arguments diminishes too. He knew the world too well. Moral justification is replaced by 'political necessity', by arguments designed to prove the expediency of injustice. Since Socrates, intellectuals of every age have exposed the fraudulence of the names given by strong men to their crimes, which is why they have always been feared and hated by those in power.

Following in the steps of Socrates, biographers of Alexander the Great have busily assembled arguments aimed at demonstrating the supreme justice – or injustice – of the king's actions. No one would have been more surprised or amused than Alexander himself to learn the reasons why he did this or that. This mode of looking at great men is, in the finest sense, humanistic. Nobody has ever been powerful enough to call the mighty to account for their actions during their lifetime, but posterity can afford to be harsher in its judgements. Truth finds readier expression in front of a king's tomb than on the steps of his throne.

Power is a spur to action. It would have been strange indeed if, having inherited a robust and healthy country and the finest army in the contemporary world, Alexander had not translated power into action. He could, of course, have abstained from the use of power, but that is the prerogative of wise old men like Diocletian and Charles V, who are weary of it. Alexander was too young not to be fascinated by its possibilities, and power became his lifelong mistress. However, he was very far from free to do as he pleased. His power was merely one star in the political firmament of his day. Within this system of co-ordinates, of effects and counter-effects, even Alexander's alternatives were limited if he wished to achieve success.

How did the political and military situation look to Alexander on his accession? His boyhood fell in the fourth century BC, a markedly revolutionary period during which faith in the power of the gods of Olympus was beginning to decline. The gods lived on in men's minds, but new horizons were unfolding beyond Homer's ancient world of myth. Even before Alexander, Hellenism had its precursors in Socrates, Plato, and Aristotle. These men ushered in a period during which Greek philosophy established an ascendancy in both East and West, while the former merely exported new religions to the latter.

In Alexander's day, the Mediterranean area embraced four large groups of Greeks who, though politically independent, were closely allied on the cultural plane. Maritime trade provided for an exchange of ideas as well as material assets. Once every four years, as for centuries past, Greeks from all over the known world converged on Olympia in the Peloponnese, there to engage in a series of artistic and athletic contests known as the 'Agon' – the Olympic Games.

The first and most important group consisted of mainland Greeks. Their days of political greatness were over. The glorious battles in which they had so valiantly and victoriously repelled the Persian Empire's onslaughts on their independence lay more than a century in the past, and were no more than nostalgic memories. Hellas had been a Macedonian protectorate ever since the battle of Chaeronea in 338 BC. The regime established by Philip II after his victory was mild in the extreme – he simply formed the cities of mainland Greece into the League of Corinth and contented himself with the status of 'captain-general' – but Macedonian garrisons occupied well-fortified strongholds at every important strategic point in Hellas.

The second group consisted of the Greeks who inhabited the west coast of Anatolia. The Ionian cities were under Persian sovereignty. No less mild than Philip II's, the Persian regime was, if anything, slightly more subtle. The Macedonians controlled Hellas by means of Macedonian garrisons, whereas the Persians maintained their authority over the Ionian Greeks through the Ionian Greeks themselves, cleverly supporting oligarchies whose interests coincided with their own. The cities enjoyed lasting peace. Trade flowed deep into Asia along secure caravan routes and the Persians allowed the oligarchs a fair share of the revenues they collected. Somewhere in the background lurked a satrap who bore responsibility for the Ionian cities to the Great King in Susa, but little was seen or heard of him.

The third major repository of Greek political power consisted of the colonies on the shores of the Sea of Marmora and the Black Sea. These maintained a wide variety of contractual relationships with the rulers of the hinterland. The cities were virtually independent, Macedonia's influence being limited to its partial command of the Dardanelles. Technically, Macedonia could bar access to the Mediterranean from the Black Sea, but the Macedonian fleet was too weak to transform this into an effective instrument of policy. Both the Persians and the Athenians were superior to the Macedonians in sea-power.

The fourth group comprised the Greek settlements in the Western Mediterranean, which were also sea-ports. In the main, these were cities in Sicily and Southern Italy, or Magna Graecia.

Another factor which Alexander had to take into account when assessing his prospects was Sparta, a military power which had not joined the League of Corinth and which maintained friendly diplomatic relations with Persia.

From Alexander's point of view, the most important political factor in the Eastern Mediterranean was the Achaemenid Empire, or Persia itself. Although there were long periods devoid of actual fighting, the centuries-old hostility between Greeks and Persians never died. Even in peacetime, the Persians persistently resorted to bribery and political intrigue as a means of fanning internal Greek strife into civil war.

Given the prevailing balance of power, the courses open to Alexander were remarkably few. Whatever schemes he devised, he was always confronted by the same foe.

It was Persia which tried to undermine the Macedonian protectorate of Hellas from within by supporting the champions of Greek independence, all of whom were, by definition, enemies of Macedonia. It was the Persians whose fleet dominated the Aegean and could blockade Macedonia's handful of harbours at any time. It was the Persians who maintained an alliance with Sparta. With Sparta's powerful military backing, Hellas might easily be seduced into open rebellion against Macedonia – a fear which materialized later on, when Alexander had already thrust deep into Asia. Finally, it was the Persians whose immense war potential represented such a constant threat to Macedonia. Anatolia, which was dominated by the Persians, was the best possible base of operations for an attack on Macedonia. Alexander would have derived little benefit from establishing a defensive position and reinforcing his authority within its confines. Macedonia could never hope for a more favourable distribution of power, so the country's security was permanently jeopardized. The Achaemenid Empire had recovered from a long spell of external weakness occasioned by internal strife. The Persians had reconquered Egypt and put down the rebellious satraps who had threatened the monarchy. Under Darius III, Persia had regained much of its original power and prestige.

Alexander, ruler and military leader of a small race of farmers and herdsmen, resolved to attack the Achaemenid Empire, the first real empire in history. This decision has laid him open to repeated charges of youthful irresponsibility. In fact, it was the product of careful political and military planning initiated by Philip II, a cool and calculating exponent of *Realpolitik*, but the young man's plan of action may certainly be described as bold, and boldness always goes beyond calculation. Never has power so greatly affected the destiny, not of one individual or race, but of the whole world.

It might have been expected that Alexander would win the acclaim of the mainland Greeks by attacking the Achaemenid Empire, but this was not so. Although he tried to invest his Persian campaign with a Panhellenic character, this was a hopeless undertaking. To the mainland Greeks, and to the Athenians in particular, there was no point in Alexander's liberating them from their Persian foe as long as he himself remained an obstacle to their freedom. As patriots, they were bound to wish him ill, and they did.

Alexander's Greek confederates were drawn mainly from Anatolia and the islands. Although devoid of Panhellenic sentiments, they did not regard Macedonian control of the mainland as a burden. What was more, the Greeks of the Aegean and Ionia were intellectually better equipped, thanks to centuries of intimate contact with the ancient civilizations of the Near and Middle East, to meet the demands of the new age that was now dawning.

Alexander preserved a lifelong admiration for Athens as the hub of Greek culture. The Athenians responded with hatred, gibes and derision, and the derision of the Agora was brilliant in its malice. The Macedonian king revenged himself on his admired Athenians in a singular way. He compelled them to forgo one of their favourite vices, to wit, controversy, which was the daily bread of their political life. They were forced to take back those who had been exiled during the savage domestic disputes of recent years. Since exile was normally coupled with the confiscation of property and its transfer to others, this decree inevitably led to endless trouble and confusion. As captain-general of the League of Corinth, Alexander would not have had the right to issue such an edict but, being by then worshipped as Pharaoh of Egypt, he claimed divine status in Hellas too, and it was as a god that he decreed the amnesty. He never demanded divine worship from the Persian Empire, so his insistence on divine status in Hellas carried no hint of megalomania – it was just another political expedient. Besides, the Greek gods were not credited with transcendency; two centuries before Alexander's time, Hecataeus of Miletus had called gods immortal human beings and human beings mortal gods. The Persian deity Ahuramazda, by contrast, did possess that measure of transcendency which the monotheistic religions of the East were entitled to claim for their single godheads. The king's appreciation of this subtle metaphysical difference shows how attentively he had listened to his tutor Aristotle as a boy.

The hostility of the mainland Greeks was supplemented by the indifference of the Greeks of Magna Graecia and the Black Sea. The Black Sea Greeks were concerned solely to avoid disruption of trade, and the Greeks of Italy and Sicily cherished equally little sympathy for Panhellenic ideas. Alexander never established close links with either group; when his brother-in-law, King Alexander of Epirus, tried to mould Magna Graecia into a great power in the Western Mediterranean, the Italiote cities proved quite as incapable as the mainland Greeks of abandoning their jealous struggles for power in favour of a broader political idea. Alexander of Epirus was murdered, and his successor Pyrrhus of Epirus came to grief a short while later, to be supplanted by the Romans.

The only Greeks to show gratitude to Alexander the Great were those of Anatolia, whom he freed from Persian domination. In return, the Macedonian king made them his allies. With him, political considerations always outweighed the urge to exploit acquired power. Thus, Ionia played a major role in his personality cult from the outset. As though in requital for the enthusiasm with which the Ionians acclaimed Alexander's plans and feats of arms, it was they who later enjoyed the lion's share of the glorious future to which he led Greek civilization. The Athenians, who had wanted nothing to do with him, were compelled, shortly after his death, to relinquish the central role in Greek culture which they had occupied for so long and with such brilliance. Alexandria, founded in Egypt by Alexander himself, became the cultural capital of Hellenism.

There is only one other man whose achievements merit comparison with Alexander's: that man is Julius Caesar.

Caesar's conquest of Gaul set the seal on the growth of the Roman Empire and his annexation of Egypt was a continuation of Alexander's work. Through him, Hellenism, that amalgam of Greek and Oriental ideas, began to infiltrate the Western Mediterranean. Between them, Alexander and Caesar paved the way for Christianity.

Julius Caesar's potent mind seethed with other plans of even greater scope. Plutarch tells us that he proposed to conduct a major campaign northwards along the western shores of the Caspian, thereby taking the barbarians of Eastern Europe in the rear and incorporating them, like the Gauls of the West, in the Roman Empire. One cannot but marvel at the brilliance of this scheme. Caesar had resolved to subdue the very area where forces were developing which later led to the downfall of the Roman Empire. Caesar was assassinated, but if he had succeeded in carrying out his plan he could have outrivalled Alexander.

Napoleon, too, has frequently been compared with Alexander, though with scant justification. The fact that he won numerous battles pales into insignificance beside his defeats at Leipzig and Waterloo. The failure of his attack on Russia is equally insignificant because success would have been just as meaningless. Alexander introduced the East to Greek culture, and Caesar did the Gauls the inestimable favour of compelling them to become part of Mediterranean civilization. If he had remained victorious, what fruits of war and peace would Napoleon have brought to the Russians?

History can point to only one other man – a man of words rather than action – whose achievements gave birth to a power structure comparable in size and historical importance with Alexander's empire. This is the prophet Mohammed. Alexander founded an empire of the spirit with drawn sword, whereas Islam began as a spiritual movement and used the sword to carve out an empire of temporal power. However, not even the Arabs, who pushed eastwards to the limits of Alexander's former dominions, succeeded in ousting the spirit of Greece.

Modern historians eschew hero-worship. It is understandable, therefore, that they should find it hard to attribute effects of such epoch-making and world-wide significance to one individual.

There have been many attempts to salvage Alexander's achievements from the domain of myth and miracle and subject them to the sober light of reason. We are repeatedly told of the 'vast and crumbling'

Persian Empire, yet the finest army in the contemporary world, organized into the invincible phalanx and commanded by one of the most brilliant generals of all time, took nearly a decade to bring this 'crumbling' colossus to its knees.

Again, many experts assert that the eastward spread of Greek ideas was a historical process which began long before Alexander and would in any case have resulted in the Hellenization of the East. We know, principally from coin finds that the eastward trend via Macedonia did, in fact, antedate Alexander's conquests. Nevertheless, the relationship between East and West is not static, nor was it even in prehistoric times. When the tide had flowed far enough in one direction, it turned. After centuries of importing Greek education, Greek vases and wine, the East began to export to the West – *inter alia* – silk, ivory, camel hair, and the concept of compassion. The process went so far that a Syrian priest of Baal ascended the imperial throne of Rome, and the whole of the Western world adopted a religion which had originated in the East. Alexander's ship of destiny may have run before the wind under full canvas, but the natural tensions between East and West would never have wrought such revolutionary changes as those which resulted from Alexander's personal intervention in history.

The army which won Alexander's victories was not only an instrument of power but a historical arena in itself. We do not know exactly when Alexander decided to succeed the Achaemenids on the throne of Persia. We can only say that, from the beginning of the campaign, none of his measures was inconsistent with such an intention.

Globe showing the extent of Alexander the Great's empire at his death. The hatched area represents the territory which he inherited from his father, King Philip II. No one would have been more astonished by this map than Alexander himself. If he really planned to gain control of the whole world, the sight of this globe would have deterred him.

Alexander was both a visionary and a realist, the very combination which so greatly contributed to his success. A future which makes political sense cannot materialize unless it has first been imagined, for imagination is a prerequisite of all historical achievement. Realists of Alexander's intellectual calibre are probably incapable of indulging in dreams whose fulfilment lies beyond the bounds of possibility. The vision of a marriage between Hellenic and Iranian culture did contain the seeds of fulfilment.

After the defeat of Persia at the battle of Gaugamela, the king began to translate his vision into reality. Without introducing many changes, he resuscitated the excellent Achaemenid civil service, whose activities had been only briefly interrupted by the war. He also trained Persian contingents for enrolment in the Macedonian army. Turks and Mongols entered his service and Asiatics were recruited as cavalry-men for use in his campaign against the steppe-dwelling nomads of Bactria and Transoxiana. During the Indian campaign, the army acquired a new weapon in the shape of elephant squadrons. Despite the Macedonians' lingering sense of pride and superiority, common hardships, battles and victories gradually welded the army's racial hotchpotch into a community that set the pattern for the cities which Alexander founded everywhere he went. Of the unifying constituents of the army which had a bearing on the growth of Hellenism, one was the baggage train which accompanied it. This included sutlers who supplied the troops with wine, merchants who changed loot into cash, money-lenders who advanced credit on future spoils of war, quacks who enabled the soldier to dispense with the services of army physicians, mobile field hospitals which transported and tended sick and wounded soldiers on the march, musicians and tumblers who provided dancing and entertainment, and the personal attendants of the great, who lived in Oriental luxury when no fighting was in progress. Also among the camp-followers were builders and crafts-men who planned to settle in Alexander's new cities in the hope of enriching themselves more quickly there than in overpopulated Hellas. Last but not least, there were girls.

Possessing no information about this picturesque train, we can only make inferences about its composition from traditional sources. Traders in loot continued to follow the world's armies for as long as looting remained a victor's prerogative. In view of the sums they advanced to the army, the money-lenders ought really to be called bankers. When Alexander decided to settle these liabilities at Susa, it turned out that his veterans were in debt to the impressive tune of roughly £7 million. That large numbers of women were an integral part of the train can be deduced from the fact that Alexander had no difficulty in finding Persian brides for ten thousand of his veterans at the mass wedding in Susa. Ten thousand girls stood ready to hand behind his phalanx of conquering heroes.

Alexander's court was a combination of military headquarters and civil administrative machine, not an isolated unit but part of a socio-logical framework. The army and its train formed the base, while the court provided the social superstructure. The mobile residence from which Alexander ruled his growing empire was the cell from which Hellenism emanated. It spread with remarkable speed; the Septuagint, or Greek translation of the Old Testament, was produced at the university of Alexandria only fifty years after Alexander's death. Hellenism eventually conquered the entire Mediterranean area. When Romans negotiated with Carthaginians, both sides spoke Greek. It was a Greek envoy sent by King Attalus II of Pergamum who broke his leg in Rome and whiled away the tedium of convalescence by composing the first Latin grammar. Caesar's fateful words at the Rubicon were not *Alea iacta est* but Ἀνερρίφθω κύβος. The die was cast in Greek, not Latin. It was Caesar's thorough grounding in Greek which enabled him to overcome the prejudices of Rome's senatorial oligarchy. Educated Romans continued to speak Greek until well into the Imperial era, preachers in the Christian churches of Rome were still using Greek in the second century, and today, when a budding classicist sighs over the grammatical complexities of the aorist, he heaves a Hellenistic sigh.

No royal court in the history of the West has ever outshone the court of Alexander the Great. Its ephemeral structure derived weight and importance from a profusion of brilliant personalities. At a time when Athens was beginning to lose its long established reputation as the centre of Hellenic intellectual life and Alexandria's fame was still in its infancy, Alexander's court represented the focus of Greek culture. There can be no clearer indication of the young Macedonian king's status or of his wide-ranging personality and profound in-fluence on other people.

The kernel of the royal household was, of course, the military head-quarters. The number of gifted generals in the king's service is an eternally surprising feature, and one which raises the problem of generations. Forty years ago, Pinder demonstrated in the field of art history that inexplicable clusters of talent appear at specific and closely defined periods. This applies not only to artistic ability but to all forms of talent. Macedonia produced two accumulations of military ability within the space of two generations. What makes this even more surprising is that their representatives all came from a single caste, the Macedonian military nobility. Philip II had enjoyed the services of a large number of first-rate military associates. Some of them served his son with equal distinction – Parmenion as chief of staff, Antipater as governor of Macedonia, and Cleitus as commander of the Companion cavalry. The younger generals with whose aid the king conducted his campaign were so numerous that a detailed account of their exploits would be virtually equivalent to an account of that campaign.

Alexander's achievements become comprehensible only when viewed in relation to his abundance of able, efficient and enthusiastic associates. His self-confidence was such that he could delegate responsibility without qualms. As a result, talented young men were repeatedly entrusted with tasks which enabled them to demonstrate their ability. Being an expert wielder of power, Alexander knew how to reward men for their services. The Macedonian army had a long-established and traditional system of ranks and titles which Alexander used as a means of assuaging the vanity of ambitious generals. He was a good enough judge of military ability to bestow honours fairly, and, where similarity of achievement rendered this difficult, ingenuity came to his aid. Hephaestion was a personal friend, Craterus a close confidant and adviser. Both men possessed major military virtues and were naturally jealous of one another – a dangerous state of affairs in view of their volatile temperaments. Alexander appointed Hephaestion Φιλαλέξανδρος or 'friend of Alexander' and Craterus Φιλοβασιλεύς or 'friend of the king'. However, it was not the prospect of honours and riches which bound Alexander's associates to him, but the unfailing magnetism of his grand designs – ventures in which a man could show his true mettle. To them, Alexander was the future.

It is a remarkable fact, and one which aroused comment even among the writers of antiquity, that none of Alexander's younger generals emerged as a dominant figure during his lifetime. They were all competent and courageous commanders who proved equal to any task Alexander set them, but it was not until after the death of their lord and master that they revealed their true stature. Hence, we are suddenly confronted by formidable figures like Ptolemy I Soter, who founded an Egyptian dynasty which endured until the death of Cleopatra; Seleucus I Nicator, who took possession of Alexander's conquests in Asia; and Antigonus, in Alexander's day 'a pale shadow;

20

later, the mightiest of the Diadochi, distinguished by his full and active career, wide-ranging influence, and heroic death at the battle of Ipsus' (Berve).

Quite as splendid as Alexander's military headquarters was his civil court. The leading administrator was Eumenes, a Greek from Cardia, a town situated in the Thracian Chersonese. Eumenes was the senior member of Alexander's chancellery. The respect felt by educated Hellenes for their own language is neatly expressed by his title. As 'Αρχιγραμματεύς or 'archgrammarian', he was editor-in-chief of the Ephemerides, a journal which recorded the progress of Alexander's campaign. Ptolemy, who wrote a biography of Alexander when he became king of Egypt, drew on the Ephemerides for material. It seems that the journal was published, but none of it survives today.

Being a Greek, Eumenes aroused increasing hostility among the Macedonian generals as he rose in the king's esteem. His most dangerous enemy was the arrogant and quick-tempered Hephaestion. Despite their enmity, Eumenes pleased the king by according Hephaestion special honours after his death at Ecbatana. He was a man of polished manners and spotless character. At Susa, Alexander married him off to Artonis, sister of his morganatic wife Barsine and widow of Memnon of Rhodes, his erstwhile adversary in the Aegean. Eumenes remained true to the king after his death. He focused all his energies on preserving the legitimate succession, but in vain. Hounded by the hatred of his enemies, he ultimately died in tragic circumstances.

Alexander's royal household included philosophers, artists, men of letters, poets, and a whole staff of scholars. Thanks to his liberal education, high standard of artistic appreciation and keen interest in science, he was able to captivate a wide variety of minds. He was also lucky enough to be a contemporary of many gifted artists and scientists. Revolutionary events had coincided with the emergence of powerful forces in the world of art. It was a time brimming with remarkable achievements in every sphere of life.

We do not know what use Alexander would have made of his authority over the empire which fate bestowed on him. Death set an untimely seal on all his plans for the future, including the last one of which we have any knowledge. Nearchus had explored the sea-route from the mouth of the Indus to the Persian Gulf. Alexander proposed to open up the sea-route between the Persian Gulf and the Red Sea, and devoted the last months of his life to preparations for this venture. It was less a military campaign than a large-scale journey of exploration undertaken in strength. We cannot but regret that the project never materialized. If it had, the Greeks would have become acquainted with the east coast of Africa and founded colonies there. Their insatiable curiosity would have driven them farther and farther southwards. By the time of the Emperor Augustus, they might well have reached Madagascar. As it was, the first European to see Madagascar loom up on the horizon was a Portuguese who had circumnavigated Africa, bound for the treasures of India.

The last act of the great warrior-king was to open a canal designed to improve the irrigation of the land bordering the middle reaches of the Euphrates. He spent a considerable time in the flooded areas, so it may have been there that he caught the malaria which killed him.

Although Alexander's empire started to disintegrate as soon as fate removed him from his seat of power, his ideas continued to dominate the world. His vision of a community of Hellenic ideas and culture encompassing both East and West became a marvellous reality in the centuries that followed.

Gold medallion from Tarsus, bearing the head of Alexander the Great

ALEXANDER THE GREAT is a historical figure of the first magnitude. Droysen opens his classic work *Geschichte Alexanders des Grossen* with the sentence: 'The name Alexander signifies the end of one world era and the beginning of another.' A hundred and thirty years of continuing historical and archaeological research have done nothing to invalidate this statement.

Alexander transformed the world in a glamorous, heroic, and picturesque way. It is only natural, therefore, that the world should wish to know what sort of man he was, what talents he possessed, what ideas animated him, what plans preoccupied him, what motives determined his actions, what his views were on art, politics and science, and what beliefs he held.

There are numerous descriptions of the course of events. Even though no contemporary account survives, much first-hand information has come down to us through the medium of later works. Prolonged and discriminating research has enabled modern authorities to tell which ancient sources are worthy of credence, so it is not hard to form a picture of Alexander's actual career. Even his contemporaries failed to agree on whether it was great and glorious or great and gruesome, whether his nature inclined more towards vice or virtue, and whether his role in history was beneficent or pernicious. Posterity has kept this controversy alive for over two thousand years. Today, verdicts on Alexander still run the gamut between boundless admiration and bitter rejection, between sympathy for his mistakes and depreciation even of his most important achievements. It is not merely curiosity that prompts people to explore the mysteries of such a unique personality. Imagination, too, comes into play. Though glamorous, heroic and picturesque enough in itself, Alexander's

career was consistently embroidered. The process began with anecdotes, those traditional stumbling-blocks of the serious historian. Of
the dozens told about Alexander, most are amusing and show the
king in a favourable light. None of them occurred exactly as told, of
course, but every one contains a germ of truth. Anecdotes focus
scattered events like a lens.

Anecdote is closely escorted by legend, which pays no heed to reality.
Legend paints its heroic portraits as it pleases, concocting fairy-tale
figures which bear no relation to the facts. Alexander legends still
survive in Ethiopia, on the Rhine, in Arabia and India. There are
still princes in the valleys of the Hindu Kush and Himalayas who
trace their own descent back to Alexander and that of their horses to
Bucephalus, the Macedonian king's famous charger. If the great man
had traversed the known world, what more natural than that legend
should send him soaring into the sky or plummeting to the ocean
bed? If the king of a small country had brought a mighty empire to
its knees, why should he not, in accordance with an age-old legendary
pattern, be the secretly reared son of the last ruler of that empire?
There thus arose the paradoxical situation in which a wholly historical
figure managed to be wholly mythical at the same time.

Admiration and rejection, curiosity and imagination – all these helped
to spread Alexander's fame. It is easy enough to sneer at fame as a
spur to action – what price glory? – but mockery misses the heart of
the matter. Fame and its golden shadow, posthumous fame, were
always regarded by the ancients as worthy of the highest endeavour.
Alexander, who was an intelligent and well-educated man, lamented
the fact that there was no Homer to hymn his achievements. This
demonstrates, first, how much more important to posterity are the
poets who extol heroic deeds than the heroes who perform them, and,
secondly, that we have little idea of the fascination exerted on the
men of the ancient world by something as ephemeral as fame. In the
seventh book of the *Iliad*, Hector, who has challenged one of the
Achaeans to a duel and is confident of victory, says:

> Greece on the shore shall raise a monument;
> Which when some future mariner surveys,
> Washed by broad Hellespont's resounding seas,
> Thus shall he say, A valiant Greek lies there,
> By Hector slain, the mighty man of war.
> The stone shall tell your vanquish'd hero's name,
> And distant ages learn the victor's fame.

The traditional values of this world were plunged into darkness by the brilliant light of a Christian metaphysic which concentrated on the world hereafter. At Mount Athos, a place already half-way to heaven, there is a picture designed to illustrate the transience of all things earthly. It shows the Patriarch of Alexandria standing before the open sarcophagus of Alexander the Great and pointing contemptuously at the pitiful skeleton which once ruled the world. Discounting the fact that Alexander's sarcophagus contained, not a skeleton, but a carefully embalmed body whose features were so well preserved that the Emperor Augustus could admire their beauty in his own day, we must admit that the Patriarch of Alexandria's Christian attitude became him well. He can scarcely have reflected that, without Alexander, there would never have been a Patriarch of Alexandria at all, but it is not feasible for us to judge people of the fourth century BC by twentieth-century standards. Our very vocabulary demonstrates how full of prejudice we are in this respect. The desire to have one's deeds hymned by Homer can only be defined by some such expressions as a thirst or craving for glory, and thirsts and cravings can hardly be described as virtues. The words alone contain that touch of condescension which pious Christians so readily feel for mortals whose souls are unsolaced by any hope of immortality. To perform great deeds for glory's sake was a passion which becomes entirely comprehensible when we remember how the ancients viewed the human condition. As long as they were limited to the prospect of a shadowy existence in Hades, posthumous fame provided a small metaphysical substitute for immortality.

There is a certain irony in the fact that it was not King Philip, himself loaded with honours, who implanted the urge to perform great deeds in his son's mind. That was done by the philosopher who was his tutor. Aristotle made Homer the basis of his royal pupil's education. A copy of the *Iliad* annotated by the great scholar accompanied Alexander everywhere on his campaigns. This royal papyrus later became one of the prized possessions of the library at Alexandria. We can trace the influence of Homer on Alexander's behaviour far into his career. Not until his world had assumed continental proportions and his strategic ideas had embraced an ocean did Homer become literature for him as well.

In addition to a desire for fame, Alexander's motives comprised a second irrational element – the πόθος referred to by all ancient writers. The basic connotations of this almost untranslatable Greek word include not only longing and yearning but regret and a painful sense of deprivation. In our context, *pothos* signifies a vague longing, a sort of cosmic curiosity, a yearning for far-off places, an urge to cross every frontier and travel to the ends of the earth. It cannot be said that this was a particularly Greek characteristic. As Plato once said, mockingly, of his fellow-countrymen: 'We squat round the sea like frogs round a pond.' Alexander's *pothos* may best be compared with the spirit of exploration typical of modern scientists who brook no frontiers in the pursuit of their aims.

The irrational elements in Alexander's character were balanced by a sovereign intellect, razor-sharp powers of discernment, cool political common sense, an acute knowledge of human nature, an inexhaustible fund of ingenuity which always enabled him to devise expedients in a crisis, and, finally, military ability. Tactically, he possessed talent of a high order; strategically, he was a genius. In action, all these qualities were subordinated to a sober evaluation of risks which verged on the pedantic. Alexander seldom erred in his assessment of a situation.

This brilliantly gifted darling of the gods was, in addition, the master of a nation which had been in the ascendant for generations – robust, youthful, and firmly attached to its monarchy. His father had bequeathed him an efficient government and an army which excelled in all the contemporary military arts. Destiny presented him with the task of settling the power-struggle between Hellas and Persia, a conflict which had dominated international relations for two centuries. Resounding though the Hellenic victories at Marathon, Salamis and Plataea had been, Persian diplomacy had always contrived to perpetuate internal Greek dissension by means of bribes and threats. The court of Susa skilfully played off Athens against Sparta and Sparta against Athens until both were exhausted. By establishing a mild hegemony over Hellas, Philip of Macedonia brought the tormented country a few years of peace. He used this period to prepare for war against Persia, and had even dispatched a small army to Anatolia under Parmenion when he fell prey to an assassin. Alexander took over his father's task and completed it. If he had failed, the course of world history would have taken a different direction. Had it not been for Alexander, as Jacob Burckhardt once said, we should know little about the Greeks and have no desire to know what little we knew. Alexander's conquest of the Persian Empire was a victory by the West over the East, Europe over Asia. It spelt the end of the Ancient Orient and the beginning of Hellenism.

Macedonia. Countryside near Kašanik. In the background, the Ljubok ▶

Alexander the Great spent his boyhood surrounded by some of the most beautiful scenery in Europe. The Macedonians among whom he grew up were free-born farmers and herdsmen. The aristocracy, or landed military nobility, kept to its estates when no campaign was in progress. The Macedonians originally inhabited the valley of the Bistritza, in the mountains on the border between Albania and Serbia. From there they debouched into the plain of Monastir and pushed on to Lake Ochrid. Geologically speaking, Ochrid is a very remarkable lake, being the remains of a Tertiary sea and possessing a fauna which became extinct elsewhere millions of years ago with the exception of the water-fleas which are still to be found in Lake Baikal. From Ochrid, the small highland people worked its way southwards to the

Macedonia. Lake Ochrid

View of the plain of Pella from Aegae, now Edessa

edge of the mountains and founded Aegae, the first Macedonian capital in recorded history. It hangs like an eyrie above the lush and fertile plain which extends from the foot of the mountains to the Gulf of Salonica. A mountain stream of clear green water flows through the still lively little township, then turns into an impressive cataract as it plunges into the depths below. Archaeologists have hazarded the theory that a cavern screened by this waterfall may contain the Macedonian royal tombs which have so far eluded discovery. Early in the seventh century BC the Macedonians set out to conquer the plain which they had only surveyed from Aegae until then. That done, they founded Pella, their second capital, on the coast. Aegae remained the hallowed heart of their kingdom, the last resting-place of their rulers, and the scene of all their major festivals.

The Macedonians did not enter Greek history until a late stage. We have no definite knowledge of them prior to the seventh century. The first Macedonian king about whom we possess reliable historical information is Amyntas I, a seventh-generation forebear of Alexander. When Darius the Great occupied Thrace during his campaign against the Scythians, it was Amyntas who sent the Great King earth and water. Although his submission was dictated by political cunning, it did, at least formally, turn Macedonia into a vassal state of Persia. Menaced by numerous enemies, the country even became a tributary

31

state of the Illyrians on its northern borders shortly before Philip II's accession. This shows how small and modest were the beginnings from which the empire of Alexander the Great eventually sprang.

Even in antiquity, controversy raged as to whether or not the Macedonians were Hellenes. They were not recognized as such by the Greeks. The problem would be solved if we had any written records of their language, but these are confined almost entirely to names. The Greeks had long looked down on the Macedonians. After Alexander's conquest of Persia the Macedonians looked down on the Greeks. This mutual condescension had its ironical side. No one did more for the Greeks, who were despised by the Macedonians, than the Macedonians, who were despised by the Greeks.

The Greeks regarded the Macedonians as barbarous because they had preserved their rustic form of government. Their king was a war-lord, and their political system, which remained wholly paternalistic until Alexander's day, had not shared in the Hellenic development of the *polis* or city-state. No attempt had been made to imitate the Greek pattern. To the Greeks, the city-state was the epitome of political wisdom – as, indeed, it proved to be during the vital centuries of Greek cultural history. It did not cost the Greeks their freedom until it had become debased. The Macedonians' arrogance, being founded on military efficiency, was the form of arrogance which makes least demands on the human intellect.

Waterfall at Aegae

Thrace. View of the ruins of Philippi, founded by Philip II

Modern authorities tend to believe that the Macedonians were among the Dorians who invaded Hellas from the north in about 1200 BC and destroyed the Mycenaean civilization. The heroes of the Iliad had sons but no grandsons. The Macedonians may have been a last wave of Dorian invaders which never reached Hellas itself. They settled in the mountains of the southern Balkans and slowly began to build up their strength, aided by a succession of energetic and politically able rulers. Philip II crowned this centuries-long process by ranging Macedonia alongside Persia, Athens and Sparta as a fourth major power in the Aegean. Philip's acquisition of Thrace was a particularly valuable addition to Macedonia's strength. Its mountains supplied tar, pitch and timber for ship-building, its mines gold and silver. In the east of the newly acquired territory the king founded a city which was named after him. Philippi was the scene of Antony's and Octavian's victory over Brutus and Cassius in 42 BC, and it later played an important role in the life of St Paul.

Archaeological research at Aegae has yet to yield results, but more and more treasures are being unearthed at Pella year by year. The spacious palace which recently came to light there could not immediately be identified, but subsequent discoveries proved that it belonged to the royal family.

It was difficult at first to decide whether the archaeologists' spades really had uncovered Pella. The site of the excavations is over twelve miles from the coast, and Pella once stood beside the sea. In fact, river-borne masses of soil and stone carried down from the mountains year after year for twenty-four centuries have pushed the coastline twelve miles out into the sea. Conclusive evidence that the place in question really is Pella exists in the form of roof-tiles stamped with the name of the city.

The mosaics unearthed in the royal palace are of very high quality. They rely for their wonderful effect on the natural colours of the pebbles of which they are made. Young Alexander must have played on these handsome and remarkably well preserved mosaic floors with his sister Cleopatra, who was one year his junior. The young princess

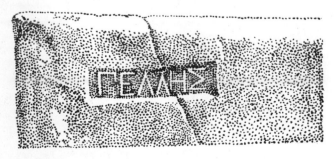

Pella. Fragment of a roof-tile stamped with the city's name

Pella. Mosaic floor in the royal palace

Pella. Pebble mosaic. A stag being attacked by a griffin

was destined to become the sole legitimate descendant of the Macedonian house, which was why, fifteen years after her brother's death, she and her son were murdered by one of the Diadochi.

The hall with the mosaic floor may also have been used for the ceremonial reception of friendly princes or envoys sent by foreign powers. One splendidly animated section depicts a stag being attacked by a griffin. There is also an elegant portrayal of Dionysus mounted on a hunting-leopard with a beribboned thyrsus in his left hand. The lion hunt (Colour Plate II) dates from a somewhat later period. This mosaic depicts an incident which probably took place near Babylon. King Alexander (left, on the defensive) is in mortal danger, but Craterus (right, with raised sword) courageously attacks the lion and kills it. One noteworthy feature of the mosaic is the nicely balanced distribution of the three figures. Using the simplest resources, the artists achieved aesthetically fascinating effects.

The profusion and quality of these works show that, although most of the artists were undoubtedly Greek, there was no reason to look down on the Macedonians. Royal Pella was by no means a backwoods provincial town.

Pella. Pebble mosaic. Dionysus riding a leopard

Pella. Pebble mosaic. Alexander and Craterus lion-hunting

Alexander I had already started to acquaint his people with Greek culture in the time of the Persian kings. He managed to gain admittance to the Olympic Games, hitherto reserved exclusively for Greeks. He also began to mint his own coins, which were of a high standard. It was Alexander I, a Macedonian, who helped to mitigate one of the worst atrocities of the Greek civil wars. Peloponnesian Mycenae was the only Greek city to have supported Athens against the Persians at the battle of Marathon by sending a contingent of hoplites, whereas the Spartans did not appear on the battlefield until victory had been won. The Mycenaeans' bravery did not dissuade the Spartans from attacking their city shortly afterwards and butchering all the inhabitants who had failed to escape. Alexander I offered the refugees asylum in Macedonia. Philip II, who had met such refugees in his youth, must surely have found this incident a striking demonstration of the fact that the political situation in Hellas constantly hovered on the brink of anarchy.

Cultural activity was centred on the Macedonian court. Perdiccas II entertained Hippocrates and Alexander I was on friendly terms with Pindar. Euripides lived at the court of King Archelaus, who even tried to get Socrates to come to Pella. Archelaus also commissioned Zeuxis to decorate his palace, thereby turning it into one of the wonders of the Greek world. Philip II employed the services of Aristotle and numbered Isocrates among his friends. Greek was spoken by members of the Macedonian nobility and, thus, by all Alexander's generals.

Philip II, Alexander's father, was a distinguished and successful statesman, a cynic and hedonist, an exponent of *Realpolitik*, an astute man brimming with energy, a big drinker, a lover of women, and a superlative soldier. Characteristic of him is the following dictum, which contains the quintessence of his political experience: 'A donkey laden with gold can scale the steepest fortress.' The gold medallion found at Tarsus shows him in the prime of life – a head imbued with dignity and majesty, somewhat idealized, rather like Zeus.

Gold medallion from Tarsus, bearing the portrait of Philip II ▶

Silver coin of Alexander I of Macedonia. Obverse and reverse

Marble head of Philip II

The sculpture in the Ny Carlsberg Glyptotek, Copenhagen, is an uncannily lifelike portrait. We do not know for certain that it represents Philip II, but stylistically it falls within the second half of the fourth century, a period when there could have been few distinguished men save Philip who presented quite such an appearance. The strong, sensual mouth, the drive and obstinacy apparent in the cheekbones, the stern and imperious gaze, the impenetrably cryptic expression, the air of mocking condescension – all these belong to Philip II. We can well imagine, too, that the man liked to laugh – perhaps too loudly on occasions. He was undoubtedly intelligent enough to have a sense of humour.

Silver coin with Philip II on horseback

Nothing redounds more greatly to Philip's credit than his friendship with Isocrates. True, he chose an excellent tutor for his gifted son in the person of Aristotle, and the world has reason to be grateful to him for that, but nothing was known of Aristotle's greatness and importance at the time of his appointment. It was different with Isocrates. Although he does not occupy the same status in our cultural pantheon as his contemporaries, Socrates, Plato and Demosthenes, he was one of the most important and influential figures in Greek history. He died a few days after the battle of Chaeronea at the age of nearly a hundred, having been born seven years before the death of Pericles. This means that his life-span corresponded to that of a man who first saw the light of day seven years before Napoleon's death and lived to see the end of the First World War.

During the 560's Athens was the centre of a school of political thought whose adherents regarded the long-term coexistence of two rival great powers as impracticable. (As we can see, modern theories are not necessarily more stupid than those of the ancient world.) Pericles, who unfortunately espoused this theory, positively drove Greece into

the Peloponnesian War, which led to the destruction of Hellenic freedom. As a matter of fact, the Greeks could only afford the Peloponnesian War because Persia's foreign policy had been crippled by
internal disorder during the decades in question. Isocrates was born
wealthy but lost his fortune when Athens was defeated. Chastened by
this bitter experience, he spent his life urging the Greeks to keep the
peace and gird themselves for war against Persia. As soon as he
realized the futility of his endeavours, he turned to Philip II, who
represented his last hope of seeing a united Hellas. Isocrates was far
removed from Plato's political utopianism. He was worldly, prag-
matical and realistic, which must have endeared him to Philip II from
the first. Like Philip, he was of the opinion that a united Greece would
appear so dangerous to the Persians that they would sooner or later
resume their attack on Hellas. Rather than be caught unawares, it
would be better to forestall them. Isocrates' ideas were undoubtedly
the subject of heated arguments at the court of Pella. Young Alexander
grew up in a politico-intellectual atmosphere in which Persia always

formed the chief topic of conversation. He was not, as Niebuhr once said, 'a splendid brigand' who set out to conquer the world for his own amusement. Heralded by the Trojan War, the conflict between East and West had a long political and spiritual prehistory.

A glance at the marble head of Isocrates tells us that he was a cultured, shrewd and benevolent man. It was he who perfected Greek prose-writing. After him, Greek education depended for its superiority on intellectual precision and formal perfection. He influenced the whole of Hellenic historical writing, both in style and approach. The battle of Chaeronea fulfilled almost all his hopes. He wrote a last letter to Philip II, congratulating him on his success, and then, a few days later, closed his eyes for the last time. Few old men can have died happier. In later years, when – to Aristotle's undoubted chagrin – Alexander began to blend Hellenic culture with Persian, the young king's thoughts may well have turned to Isocrates from time to time.

Philip conducted innumerable campaigns, principally against the mountain tribes of the Balkans, which still presented a military threat. Macedonia did Hellas the seldom appreciated service of shielding it for centuries from invasion by the barbarians of the north. However, Philip also attacked Greek cities in the Aegean during his conflicts with Athens and Sparta. An arrow-head inscribed with his name was found at Olynthus on the peninsula of Chalcidice. It is related that a bowman named Aster from Amphipolis one day offered his services to the king, boasting that he could even hit a bird on the wing. Philip laughingly replied that he would engage him when he took the field against starlings. Aster was understandably offended. While Philip was besieging Methone, the archer, who had gone over to the defenders' side, loosed off an arrow on which he had written: 'Into King Philip's right eye'. The arrow found its mark, but Philip had it returned bearing the written threat: 'When King Philip captures Methone he will have Aster hanged'. Philip II did, in reality, only have one eye, a fact which he tried to disguise at banquets by putting a gold laurel-wreath on his head and pulling it low over his forehead. The one-eyed man with the crooked laurel-wreath must have presented a sinister but majestic appearance. Plutarch describes a feast at which the king got dead drunk and quarrelled with his son. The upshot of the affair was that Alexander sought refuge with the barbarians of Illyria.

Philip's greatest opponent was the Athenian statesman Demosthenes, another man with an impressive head, though there is something almost pinched and fanatical about his face, for all its intelligence.

Arrow-head from Olynthus, bearing the name of Philip II

Demosthenes had a petty streak. He openly rejoiced at Philip's assassination, having early recognized his enemy's far-reaching aims. He bitterly and repeatedly attacked the Macedonian king in the Athenian Agora, where his celebrated speeches earned him the reputation of being the finest orator in the Greek tongue. Philip paid no attention to these speeches. He continued to exploit changes in the internal Greek balance of power for his own ends until, in a final battle, he managed to eliminate the last resistance to Macedonian domination of Hellas. The battle of Chaeronea, fought in 338 BC, marked the end of Greek independence. Crown Prince Alexander, only eighteen years old at the time, settled the outcome by leading a brilliant cavalry charge at the correct tactical moment. A massive lion erected in honour of the fallen still stands guard over the battlefield where one of the greatest generals in history won his first victory.

Chaeronea. Marble lion commemorating the battle

Marble head of Demosthenes ▶

Gold medallion from Abukir, bearing the head of Olympias

Alexander's father was far less of a problem to him in his youth than Olympias, his mother. He could more or less calculate what to expect from Philip, the bold realist, but Olympias, by contrast, was proud and capricious, intelligent and passionate, ambitious and vengeful. Originally known by the delightful name Myrtale, she came of a great family and must, by all accounts, have been a great beauty. A cameo in the Kunsthistorisches Museum at Vienna (Colour Plate I), which dates from the third century BC, portrays her with her son Alexander. It is probable that the artist based his work on earlier portraits, so we can assume that, despite obvious idealization, both heads bear a certain resemblance not only to each other but to reality. The gold medallion from Abukir is far more realistic, even though it dates from Roman times. It depicts Olympias as a beautiful, aristocratic and extremely forceful person.

Olympias was a daughter of Neoptolemus I, king of the Molossians, whose name itself is redolent of myth. Neoptolemus traced his descent back to the first bearer of that name, the son of Achilles. At the share-out of booty after the fall of Troy, Andromache, Hector's widow, was allotted to Neoptolemus as a concubine. Their son Molossus became king of Epirus. Of all those who fought in the Trojan War, Achilles was the only one whose clan survived the Dorian invasion. This was probably because the Myrmidons, Achilles' tribe, lived in such remote and inaccessible valleys in Epirus that the Dorians simply bypassed them on their southward journey to the sea.

Alexander had no reason to doubt the authenticity of his family tree. There was no sharp distinction in the Greek mind between myth and history. Even our own ultra-rationalistic historians find it impossible to draw a precise line between them and are occasionally obliged to incorporate another piece of thinly disguised myth into history. The Trojan War did take place and Achilles did exist. Enlightened as Alexander's age may have been, the ancient myths lived on. Thetis, Achilles' mother, was a nereid or sea-nymph, and Olympias was not the sort of woman to disclaim any part of a pedigree which went back to a goddess. Again, if Philip laid greater stress on his claims to descent from Heracles than accorded with his native scepticism, it may have been from a desire not to be too greatly outshone by Olympias; after all, the Trojan War was less than a thousand years old. Poets had kept the tradition alive and artists confined themselves almost exclusively to mythical themes: whether embodied in marble or bronze, mosaics, murals, paintings or decorated vases, myths were an ingredient of daily life.

Greek vase.
Heracles in combat with the Nemean lion

We can guess how Alexander's youthful imagination must have been stimulated, say, by the sight of a wine-jug depicting Heracles in combat with the lion, its hind-leg poised to inflict a mortal wound. As a distant descendant of Achilles, he must also have derived great pleasure from portrayals of the hero bandaging his wounded friend Patroclus. Alexander's own Patroclus was Hephaestion, who later became the young king's only close friend.

The beautiful Olympias loved snakes and always kept some by her. In spring-time she used to join the maenads, or female votaries of Dionysus, and roam the woods with her hair loose and thyrsus waving, as Euripides describes in the *Bacchae*. The adolescent prince must have found her a highly unsettling sort of mother. She repeatedly hinted that Alexander had been fathered by Zeus, not Philip, and – at least in later years – strengthened Alexander's own belief in his divine descent. In a letter written to her from the oasis of Siwa in the Libyan desert, Alexander mentioned that the high priest of Ammon had entrusted him with a secret which could be communicated to her alone, and that he would disclose it on his return. Olympias never learned the secret because Alexander never came home.

Philip left his son's education to the queen during the early years of their marriage, with the result that Alexander's boyhood was full of unresolved contradictions. Throughout his career, one can trace the dual impact made on him by the forceful image of his cynical but clear-sighted father, on the one hand, and, on the other, by his fascinating mother with her exciting aura of mystery. Alexander's was no easy inheritance.

Greek vase-painting. Achilles bandaging Patroclus

Where physical appearance is concerned, we possess many representations of Alexander the Great in marble and bronze, on gold and silver coins, plaquettes and cameos, yet he permitted only three artists to portray him from life – Apelles, Lysippus, and Leochares.

Alexander had become friendly with Apelles, the painter, at home in Pella. Meeting him again in Ephesus, he commissioned him to decorate the temple of Artemis there. A charming anecdote is told relating to this period. Apelles, who was renowned for his beauty of line and his *charis*, or natural grace, must have painted rather in the style of Botticelli. While working on a picture of foam-born Aphrodite emerging from the waves, a subject particularly suited to his technique, he had the misfortune to become enamoured of his model, Pancaste, one of the king's mistresses. As soon as Alexander heard, he made him a present of the beautiful girl. The germ of truth in this anecdote is not, of course, that Alexander was indifferent to women, but that he was a magnanimous man. There are many authentic instances of his generosity, but none so colourful as the story of the bequeathed mistress.

Lysippus, who was primarily an artist in bronze, once said that people should be portrayed as they appear, not as they are. He might thus be termed an impressionist. Leochares, the third of Alexander's favourite artists, was the creator of the Apollo Belvedere. Between them, the three men formed the *élite* of their age. The Renaissance was rooted in the rediscovery of Hellenistic works for Europe did not become acquainted with classical, let alone archaic, Greek art until a much later date.

Detailed descriptions of Alexander's physical appearance are given by his contemporaries. The king was a powerfully built man of medium height, an excellent horseman and skilled performer at all forms of sport. His face was animated and intelligent and he always carried his head slightly on one side. Whether or not this was originally a habit, it became apparent after he sustained a neck wound during an expedition to the Danube area at the beginning of his career. There are many references to his well-groomed appearance, and we are specifically told that his clothes emitted a pleasant odour. His heterochromous eyes, one of them darker than the other, lent him a subtle air of distinction. There was something dreamy, veiled and remote about his gaze, but he was capable of sudden fits of rage. His generals were treated courteously and he showed a strong sense of humour when dealing with his soldiers. Fond of sitting over his wine until far into the night, he loved to conduct erudite or light-hearted conversations.

Alexander as a youth. Marble head from Asia Minor

Alexander breaking in Bucephalus. Bronze

All in all, he must have been a privileged member of the human race. The Louvre has a marble head of Alexander at the age of sixteen and one should not be put off by its idealized treatment, which endows the youth with great charm, appeal and intelligence. On the other hand, anyone who attempted to read his future career from his face would guess it to be that of an artist rather than a statesman and general. A bronze in the Museo Archeologico in Florence gives as loving a portrayal of Alexander as the Louvre's marble head. It shows him breaking in Bucephalus, a thoroughbred charger which had been offered to Philip II for the astronomical sum of fifteen talents – roughly £25,000 in modern terms. The Macedonians knew something about horseflesh, so the price must have been reasonable, but Philip refused to buy because nobody could handle the nervous and unruly beast. Then the young Alexander volunteered to ride it; doubt gave way to anxiety and anxiety to delight as the king and his entourage watched him subdue the horse. The bronze, less than five inches high, shows the first stage of breaking in. The animal is still shying and rearing, still rolling its eyes with terror, but it can already feel its future master's light and delicate touch. Although difficult to date closely, the bronze is probably Hellenistic. One thing that can be stated with certainty is that Bucephalus was the most famous horse in history; it carried Alexander in all his battles, accompanied him to India, and finally died beside the Hydaspes. Alexander founded a city named Bucephala in his charger's honour and the animal's memory lives on in the Hindu Kush, Himalayas, and Punjab – local peasants still venerate a Buddhist stupa near Rawalpindi as its tomb.

Buddhist stupa near Rawalpindi, venerated as the tomb of Bucephalus

Philip II appointed Aristotle to be his son's tutor. Aristotle was born
in 384 BC at Stagira in Chalcidice, a small town whose site is still
surrounded by magnificent forests. His father Nicomachus had served
as physician to the Macedonian court, so his summons to Pella may
have been partly due to this long-standing personal connection.

Next to Plato, Aristotle was the greatest mind in the history of Greek
philosophy – perhaps the highest honour which the goddess of wisdom
has ever bestowed. According to Aristotle's own definition, philosophy embraces the entirety of perceptible objects. Apart from being
a zoologist, botanist, meteorologist, astronomer, physicist, metaphysi-
cian, and moralist, he made a particularly close study of logic, the
science of reasoning. Aristotle made a vital contribution to the history
of European thought, and Western scholars drew on the springs of his
knowledge for many centuries. He even exerted an influence on the
philosophical ideas of Judaism and, later, of Islam; many of his works
would have been lost to us had they not been preserved in Arabic
translations. Avicenna, the Arab philosopher and physician, was one
of his adherents, and Thomas Aquinas was to blend Aristotelian
philosophy with Christian theology. In our own century, Aristotle

I   Onyx cameo of Alexander and his mother Olympias

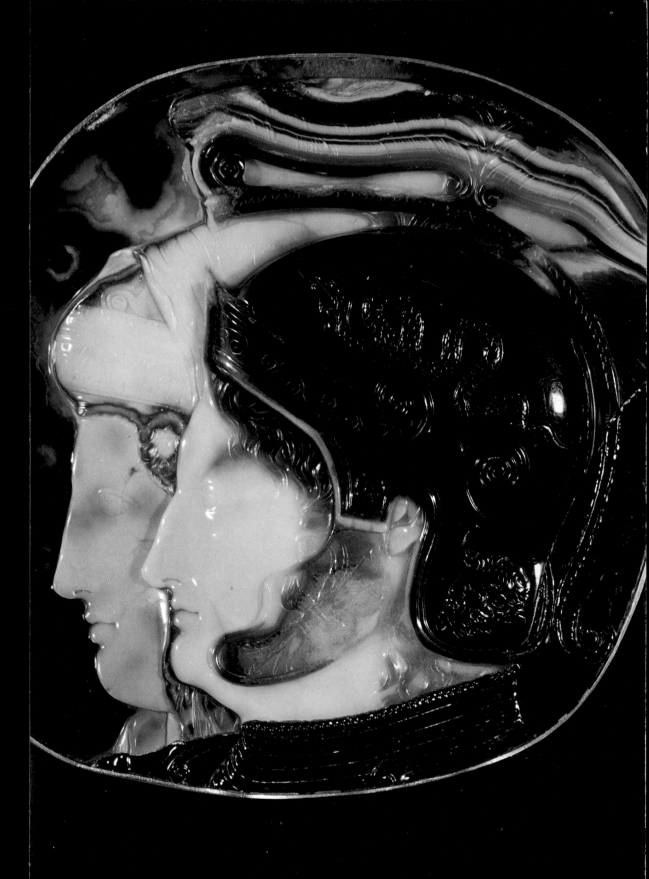

Roman mosaic from Pompeii. Plato's Academy

was rediscovered by Husserl and his pupils as the father of pheno-
menology and ontology.

At seventeen, Aristotle went to Athens and entered Plato's Academy,
where he remained until summoned to Pella more than two decades
later. A mosaic from Pompeii shows Plato surrounded by his pupils.
The master is leaning against an olive-tree, drawing in the sand with
a stick. The seated figure in front of the column is probably Aristotle,

'Plato's
olive tree' beside
the road from
Athens to Eleusis

and the Acropolis is depicted with great topographical accuracy in the top right corner. The Academy was situated some way out of Athens on the road to Eleusis. Plato's olive-tree still exists and the trunk's circumference is consistent with an age of two and a half thousand years.

It was a fortunate accident of history that Aristotle should have been appointed Alexander's tutor. He instructed the young prince in all branches of contemporary knowledge and so helped to give him a first-class education. It was also of importance that Aristotle was the sort of man whom even Alexander could look up to. The young king corresponded with Aristotle throughout his campaign, principally on scientific matters.

The basis of the prince's moral education was Homer's epic poem, the *Iliad*. Papyrus BM486D, which embodies verses 502–537 of Book XI, actually dates from the third century BC and is thus one of the earliest surviving Homeric fragments. It tells how Paris wounded the physician Machaon, whom Nestor carried off to the ships in his chariot on Idomeneus' advice, and how Cebriones urged the stalwart Hector to press forward against Ajax and his companions.

Sir Flinders Petrie, who discovered the papyrus, admits that he did not at first realize that it contained lines from the *Iliad*. This was not because the fragment is so mutilated but because several of the lines do not occur in any other known manuscript of Homer. Nearly all extant manuscripts are based on the annotated edition by Aristarchus of Samothrace, who held the chair of Homeric studies at Alexandria University about a hundred years after Alexander's death. Aristarchus' edition passed from Alexandria to Byzantium, where Homer was required reading in schools. The fact that Homer survived the Turkish conquest of Constantinople in AD 1453 was due to one man, Cardinal

Fragment of an 'Iliad' papyrus from Egypt

Bessarion. Thanks to his outstanding career, he was the only Greek Orthodox Christian to attain the rank of cardinal without renouncing the Great Schism. Born in 1400 at Trebizond, then an imperial seat, Johannes Bessarion became a monk and later archbishop of Nicaea, the place where the Christian creed acquired its final form. The Emperor John VIII Palaeologus took Bessarion with him to Rome in the hope of ending the conflict between the two great Christian Churches but when the emperor's plans foundered on the stubborn resistance of the Eastern clerics, Bessarion stayed on in Italy. Pope Eugene IV made him a cardinal and eventually promoted him Latin Patriarch of Constantinople. Bessarion's priceless library, which he brought with him to Italy, was inherited by the city of Venice on his death and among the manuscripts it contained was one of the *Iliad*. Published by a Frenchman in the eighteenth century, this forms the basis of all our modern editions. Thus, we owe the preservation of the major work of antiquity's greatest poet to the erudition of a slightly unorthodox monk and the theological obstinacy of several all too orthodox prelates.

Gentile Bellini. Tabernacle door bearing a portrait of Cardinal Bessarion

*Alexander the Great.
The Azara herm*

Of all the portraits of Alexander the Great, the most important is the Louvre's so-called Azara herm, which was discovered at Tivoli. The credit for preserving it belongs to Don José Nicolo de Azara, 'His Most Catholic Majesty's Envoy Plenipotentiary to the Holy See'. For decades the doyen of the diplomatic corps in Rome, Azara was a grand seigneur, a noted man of letters, patron of the painter Raphael Mengs, and one of the first art collectors on a European scale.

Experts agree that the Azara herm is a Roman copy of a sculpture in marble by Lysippus, but even as a copy it possesses considerable artistic merit. It accords very closely with Plutarch's description of Lysippus' most famous work, 'Alexander Carrying a Spear'. Every line of it betrays the hand of an artist whose splendid model has inspired him to scale the heights of artistic achievement. The Azara herm bears the inscription:

ΑΛΕΞΑΝΔΡΟΣ ΦΙΛΙΠΠΟΥ ΜΑΚΕ(ΔΩΝ)

ALEXANDER THE MACE(DONIAN), SON OF PHILIP

The broken statue found at Priene in a building dedicated to the cult of Alexander, and now in the Staatliche Museen in Berlin, dates from the late fourth century BC and thus originated in the years immediately following Alexander's death. The figure's left hand, here detached, holds a sword. Roughly one-third life-size, this piece does not possess the same artistic merit as the Azara herm but compensates by its robust realism.

Another work, unearthed at Alexandria, and now in America, dates from a later period, the second century BC. Its delicacy of feature and the somewhat over-sentimentalized set of the head render it typical of the high romantic phase of Hellenistic sculpture.

Alexander the Great.
Marble head from Egypt

The head of Alexander visible in the rather smaller reproduction has had a chequered career. It both exists and does not exist. The sculpture was obviously copied from a work which bore a strong resemblance to the Pergamum head. A German painter acquired it jointly with a friend in Egypt in 1900. The painter died and his friend took the valuable piece to his house in Silesia. In 1945, before fleeing to the West, he buried it in his garden, which was a large one. Later, when he tried to plot its position, he was forced to admit that he had forgotten the spot where his buried treasure was, and he has since died. The Istanbul Museum's head of Alexander, which was found at Pergamum, is distinguished by its artistic refinement and human appeal. It dates from the time of Eumenes II, the ruler who commissioned the famous Pergamum altar, and it is probable that this piece, too, was based on Lysippus' great exemplar. The style of representation scarcely changed at all for many generations and artistically, the Pergamum head is not inferior to the Azara herm. The furrows on Alexander's brow indicate that he was slightly older than is customary in such portrayals. There is something moving about the expression of vague melancholy on the manly face.

64

Silver coin of Lysimachus.
Alexander wearing the horns of Ammon

Gold medallion from Abukir.
Alexander wearing the horns of Ammon

Silver coin of Ptolemy I.
Alexander wearing an elephant head-dress

Gold medallion from Abukir.
Alexander as a Roman emperor

Silver coin. Alexander as Heracles, with lion's skin

All the coins illustrated here belong to the fourth century BC but the medallions are from Abukir and of Roman date. Much interest attaches to them, although their fame derives from half a century of unresolved controversy. Are they, in fact, superb specimens of Roman goldsmith's work, or a series of brilliant fakes? In 1902, Parisian experts were approached by several oriental gentlemen of reportedly suspect appearance and mysterious demeanour who astonished them by producing a number of gold medallions strongly reminiscent of the Tarsus medallions, from which our earlier reproduction of Philip II's portrait was taken. The experts of the Bibliothèque Nationale distrusted the Levantines. Meeting with an equally cool reception from the numismatists of the British Museum in London, the oriental gentlemen travelled to Berlin. Heinrich Dressel, curator of the antiquities department of the Royal Numismatic Collection, bought five of their medallions for a sensational sum. Although Dressel was authoritatively regarded as an expert of international repute, the authenticity of the pieces at once became the subject of a heated debate which rages to this day. The head faces right on the coins and left on the medallions; the first pair shows Alexander wearing the horns of Ammon in token of his divine ancestor, the second shows him in an elephant head-dress reminiscent of his Indian campaign (left) and in the armour of a Roman emperor (right). On the coin above, Alexander is wearing the lion's skin of Heracles.

Gold medallion from Abukir. Alexander with shield and spear

The Abukir medallion showing Alexander with shield and spear is
almost startlingly lifelike and is one of the most remarkable portrayals
of him in existence. If genuine, it can only have been modelled on a
contemporary work which has since disappeared. After thirteen years
of war, hardship, wounds, sickness, and attempts on his life, not to
mention the death of his friend Hephaestion and all the political set-
backs he had undergone, Alexander may well have looked like this.
We can rediscover what we know of Alexander in his face, the face of
a man who, in the course of his brief royal career, 'transformed the
world'.

The god Ahuramazda on the gate of the tripylon at Persepolis ▶

II Miracle and Mystery of an Empire

THE PERSIAN EMPIRE, founded in the middle of the sixth century by Cyrus the Great of the Achaemenid dynasty, was the first real empire in history. It was not the first time that the Eastern Mediterranean had been controlled by a single large country. The Egyptians, Babylonians, Hittites and Assyrians had all acquired great-power status in their time, but the Persians were the first to create a political structure whose strength, size, permanency and general aura entitled it to be called an empire.

The Persians were Iranians who came from the steppe which runs diagonally across Eurasia from the Danube to Lake Baikal, an interminable expanse of grazing land roamed by countless nomadic tribes of which one would occasionally sally forth to conquer the civilized world. Being a branch of Indo-European, the Iranian language is related both to Greek and Sanskrit. The Persians entered the Ancient Orient, the scene of their major role in history, at about the turn of the first millennium BC, and slowly pushed southwards where the beginning of their climb to power saw them in Persis, the fertile heart of their empire-to-be. They were a young race invading a world of ancient tradition; not only was it an old world, but – as Olmstead points out with the sort of sudden insight which can light up whole horizons – it *knew* that it was old. Nothing could have been more surprising than that the conquerors, far from being barbarians, actually brought cultural enrichment.

The Persian Empire was less than half a century in the making and it ultimately extended from the borders of Ethiopia in the south to the Caucasus, Caspian Sea and Aral Sea in the north, from the shores of the Mediterranean in the west to the Indus Valley in the east. Cyrus and Darius the Great were the architects of this empire whose handiwork endured for two hundred years.

It was only natural, in view of its immense size, that there should always be trouble somewhere in the empire – defection in border territories, revolts by savage mountain tribes, rebellious satraps, and, as if that were not enough, the murderous intrigues that almost traditionally beset every new accession to the throne. However, there were very few full-scale wars during the two centuries in question, which brought peace, prosperity and security to a large number of races. The Pax Achaemenica was one of the happier epochs in human history.

The Persians' success, though miraculous at first sight, does not defy explanation. Their innate talent for political organization was a legacy of the steppe, but they also had that endearing symptom of youthful freshness, a respect for tradition. Their happy combination of these two attributes prompted them to test every hallowed tradition for political expediency which accounts for their attitude towards religion, a field in which Europe can show little to compare with their spirit of liberalism and toleration.

Religious toleration was something entirely new to the world, since every victor felt it incumbent upon him to present the deities who had aided his victory with as many new devotees as possible. The peoples of the Ancient Orient suffered changing masters and changing gods with equanimity. Centuries of tribulation, danger, war and insurrection, together with a stoicism born of drought and disease, had endowed them with a boundless capacity for enduring misfortune, particularly of the kind that stemmed from misgovernment. Their patience made them easy to govern as long as their rulers did not oppress them unduly and the Persians were sensible enough to be mild, their mildness was in pleasant contrast to the brutality of the Assyrians, who had recently been defeated by the Babylonians. Cyrus, who allowed the children of Israel to leave Babylon, where they had been held in captivity by the Assyrians, was even referred to as the Lord's Anointed by Isaiah. Jehovah declared that HE had held the king's right hand so as 'to subdue nations before him'.

The architects of the Persian Empire built it with a great future in mind. What they feared least about that future, in all probability, was that its very excellence would help the conqueror of their empire to prevail. On the other hand, it was Alexander's brilliant grasp of Cyrus' and Darius' political wisdom and his attempt to reconcile victors and vanquished which enabled the spirit of Persia to survive the Macedonian conquest. Unique though Alexander was and clearly though the world-wide transformation achieved by him bore the stamp of his exceptional personality, his political approach was so sublimely un-prejudiced that he never balked at learning from his enemies. Having gauged the strength and vitality of the Persian administrative machine from his own efforts and endeavours, Alexander had good reason to admire it, he had to fight for more than a decade to bring it down, yet before the struggle was over he restored those of Darius I's political institutions which had ceased to function as a result of the war. He made no immediate changes in the satrapies into which the vast empire was divided. Indeed, in many cases he entrusted viceregal power to the very satraps who had exercised it under Darius III. He also took over the existing civil service, consisting of Elamites, Babylonians and Syrians, which had functioned so well under Persian rule. In true bureaucratic fashion, it continued to function excellently under Alexander and even under his successors, the Seleucids. Ara-maic remained the language of officialdom, as it had been in the Achaemenid Empire, it thus became the *lingua franca* of the East for centuries to come, just as Greek later became the κοινή of the Mediter-ranean area and Latin the language of officials, clerics and scholars in medieval Europe. Although versed in the Hebrew scriptures, Jesus spoke Aramaic in his daily life and the language survives to this day. It occurs in parts of the Jewish liturgy, is used by the Syrian Church, and can still be heard in villages in the Anti-Lebanon, in South-East Anatolia, and on the eastern shores of Lake Urmia in Armenia. Its widely scattered traces are an indication of its former international currency.

The most important feature of the old empire to be retained by Alexander was the monarchical tradition, which had passed without a break from the Medes to Cyrus. Alexander, himself of royal blood, respected his adversary's status and Darius III, who had been murdered by his own men, was buried with royal honours at Alexander's behest. Later, Alexander married Princess Stateria, Darius' daughter. Any son of this marriage would have been legitimate heir to the charisma of the Macedonian and Persian kings.

One of the mysteries of the Achaemenid Empire is its art. Although a youthful people of great artistic ability, the Persians produced no new and enduring art once they had established themselves as a world power. They were impressed – too impressed, perhaps – by the ancient works of art which they encountered as conquerors. Achaemenid art is a mixture of Elamite, Mesopotamian and ancient Aryan elements, though the Persians brought it to a wonderful degree of perfection. Persepolis, one of the finest and most considerable monuments

*III   Lapis lazuli head of an Achaemenid prince from Persepolis,
probably Xerxes, the son of Darius the Great*

bequeathed to us by the ancient world, was built about a generation earlier than the Periclean Acropolis, although, curiously enough, the Greeks did not know of the existence of this imperial seat until Alexander's day. The far-reaching effects of Achaemenid monumental art are evident in the vast Mauryan empire founded by Chandragupta shortly after Alexander's appearance in the Punjab. Chandragupta was an Indian prince who had been profoundly impressed by Alexander when he visited him in his camp beside the Hydaspes as a youth and, in a strange way, the maharajah helped to decide the outcome of the wars of succession which followed Alexander's death. Elephants presented by Chandragupta to King Seleucus after a trial of strength with him settled the outcome of the battle of Ipsus in 301 BC, which led to the final dissolution of Alexander's empire. The influence of Persian works of art on a small scale can also be identified among the Scythians and as far afield as Eastern Siberia but Achaemenid art never acquired any major importance from the Western point of view. It remained what it had been from the outset, undergoing no changes in the two centuries that elapsed between the construction of Persepolis by Darius I and its occupation by Alexander. One has only to compare what happened in Greece during the same period to see that, although Achaemenid art was ancient and beautiful, it had the sterile beauty of a dying era.

The mystery of the succeeding centuries is quite inexplicable. Five hundred years after Alexander's day, when the golden age of Hellenism was past and the Romans had extended the frontiers of their empire to the Euphrates, Persia awoke to new life. This time, the burgeoning political strength of the Sassanid Empire was accompanied by an extraordinarily rich regeneration of Persian art which exerted a profound influence on Europe. The ceremonial of the Sassanid court, part of which dated from Achaemenid times, penetrated to the princely courts of Europe via Byzantium, and the medieval code of chivalry also originated in the same quarter. The gifted Persian people astounded the world with its creative vitality for yet a third time. Admittedly, the Mohammedan Arab conquest of Persia interrupted the creative flow for several centuries, just as Alexander's conquest had done, but the renaissance of Persian art in the ninth century AD was of such overwhelming splendour that Frye christened this period the Persian 'conquest' of Islam.

IV   Gold rhyton in the form of a winged lion, from Ecbatana.
This rare piece dates from the turn of the fifth–fourth centuries BC,
in the golden age of Achaemenid art   73

The plain of Pasargadae in Persis, showing the tomb of Cyrus the Great ▶

The surviving relics of Cyrus the Great, founder of the Persian Empire, include a sculptural representation of his left foot, his tomb, and his posthumous fame. His capital was in Persis, in the highland plateau of Pasargadae where the country-side is barren but magnificent. Travelling across the Iranian highlands, whether by camel, car or aeroplane, one always gains the impression that the country consists entirely of arid mountains, nevertheless, wherever water exists, a 'paradise' blooms. 'Paradise' is the Persian word for garden. Although virtually bare of trees today, the plateau of Pasargadae used to be one huge park dotted with palaces. The fragmentary sculpture of Cyrus the Great was uncarthed when the foundations of the palace were excavated, where now a solitary winged genie still gazes out over the plain; its four-winged motif recurs in the archangels in Byzantine mosaics. The palaces were sumptuously decorated, and there was something genuinely imperial about their spacious lay-out.

Pasargadae. Fragment of a sculpture of Cyrus the Great

Pasargadae. Tomb of Cyrus the Great

Cyrus' tomb at Pasargadae has survived the passage of time comparatively unscathed. Although empty today, the vault is the only existing edifice in the world of which it can be said with certainty that Alexander the Great actually set foot inside. It was neglected when he arrived at Pasargadae, so he ordered it to be restored and entrusted it to the care of several magi. When he learnt, on his return from India, that the magi had failed to carry out his orders, he punished them severely.

The tomb was rediscovered in 1638 by some envoys dispatched to Shah Sufi by Queen Christina of Sweden. The drawing below was the first illustration of the famous building ever to reach Europe. It is easily recognizable despite the touchingly naive way in which the artist has Europeanized it, though the number of steps does not tally.

Strangely enough, nomadic tribesmen believe the monument to be the tomb of King Solomon's mother. Passing the place on their spring and autumn treks, they take the tribe's lead-camel round the tomb three times with ritual solemnity and smear the stone steps with mare's milk and honey. How and when this custom came into being is unknown but it is a curious fact that a number of extant ancient monuments in the Near East preserve some folk-memory such as this. Many Biblical characters, e.g. Solomon and Moses are mentioned in the *Koran*.

Pasargadae. Scandinavian envoys discovering the tomb in 1638

The two fire-altars at Pasargadae date from the time of Cyrus and are of particular archaeological interest. They have never been excavated, but stand as they have always stood, silently decaying in a flower-strewn meadow watered by a small stream. One wonders how much of them will survive the next two and a half thousand years.

The Zagros Mountains, which run in a south-south-easterly direction for about seven hundred miles, separate Mesopotamia, the lowland area traversed by the Euphrates and Tigris, from the Iranian highlands. The peaks of this rugged mountain chain rise to a height of 15,000 feet, or almost that of Mont Blanc. The Zagros are a mountain retreat whose inaccessible valleys are inhabited by the remnants of numerous defeated peoples. Having sought and found refuge in the wilderness, they relive their ancient glories by retelling the tales of old. In many places, when the grass of the steppe begins to wither, nomads drive their herds up into the lush green alpine meadows.

Pasargadae. Fire-altars dating from the time of Cyrus

The 'Gateway of Asia' in the Zagros Mountains

There is a break in the Zagros Mountains at Bisutun (Behistun), roughly in the middle of the range. The Persians, who had learnt how to build roads in Mesopotamia, used this convenient pass to link Babylon with Ecbatana. This stretch later became part of the famous 'Silk Road' along which camel trains used to transport bales of the precious material from China to the Mediterranean. The Bisutun Pass is known as the Gateway of Asia and countless generals, both victorious and vanquished, have passed through it with their armies in the course of the centuries. The first was Queen Semiramis of Babylon and the last Ahmed Pasha, who occupied Ecbatana for the Sultan of Turkey in 1731. It was at this historic spot that Darius I

81

The cliffs of Bisutun seen from the south-east ▶

chose to immortalize himself, carving into a precipitous wall of rock almost two hundred feet above the caravan route a relief showing a defeated rebel being led into his presence. An inscription enumerates the king's achievements and recounts in detail how Darius ended the wars of succession after the death of Cambyses. A magus named Gaumata, perhaps the most successful swindler in history, had secured the throne by false representation – Darius, a true Achaemenid of the royal line, placed himself at the head of a group of his supporters and killed Gaumata. Then, with a series of swift and decisive strokes worthy of Alexander the Great himself, he rescued the empire from the anarchy into which it was fast subsiding.

For all its monumentality and archaic simplification, the Bisutun relief clearly shows Darius to have been a born ruler. A man of majestic appearance, he performed mighty deeds, both in peace and war, he conquered the Punjab, or land of the 'five rivers', and may even have reached the Ganges. Nothing could be more unfair than to describe Alexander's invasion of India as a romantic escapade. The Punjab was one of the richest areas in the Achaemenid Empire, and the Indian satrapy delivered three hundred and sixty talents of gold dust in taxes alone – a vast sum. Alexander merely implemented the sweeping strategic plans of his successful predecessor. Two centuries of peace proved how right both Darius and Alexander were; it was not Alexander's fault that an untimely death cut short the consolidation of his conquests – the Seleucids, who succeeded him, completed that task shortly afterwards. Bactrian Greeks also reached the Ganges four centuries after Alexander, and Indian art remained under Greek influence for many hundreds of years.

Like Cyrus before him, Darius founded cities in the marches of Bactria so as to protect the territory between the Oxus and the Jaxartes from incursions by ever-aggressive mounted tribes from the steppes of Central Asia. Alexander, following his example in this respect too, found that the fortifications built by Cyrus were still intact. Here, too, subsequent disasters confirmed the wisdom of his precautionary measures.

The Persian king moved into Europe and secured a grip on the northern coast of the Aegean by occupying Thrace. Amyntas of Macedonia, as we have previously mentioned, had already sent him earth and water in token of submission, and, during a campaign against the Scythians, Darius actually crossed the Danube. Having marched along the northern shores of the Black Sea, he reached the Volga in the vicinity of modern Stalingrad. A relic of this military progress is

Bisutun relief, detail. Head of Darius the Great

a fragment of a clay tablet bearing ancient Persian cuneiform characters recently unearthed in Rumania.

The Greeks of the mainland had supported the Ionian cities of Asia Minor in a revolt against the Persians and the Great King decided to teach them a lesson, but his expeditionary force was defeated at Marathon. This was not the earliest occasion of strife between Persians and Greeks, however, because the dispute over the Ionian cities went back to the time of Cyrus. The Persians and Greeks were hereditary foes for whom, fundamentally, even the Trojan War had represented a conflict between Asia and Europe.

Mighty as the military achievements of Darius the Great may have been, his role as a peacemaker was still more important. From the Punjab he sent an expedition down the Indus to explore the sea route from its estuary to Egypt. He decreed the building of a 'Suez Canal' which would link the Nile and, thus, the Mediterranean, with the Red Sea. He divided the empire into satrapies, twenty-nine of which are listed in his funerary inscription. He reorganized the civil service on such efficient lines that Alexander was able to utilize it with success. He built roads, established the first postal service – yet another Persian invention – and fostered trade. Emulating the great Hammurabi, he decreed the compilation of a legal code. He introduced the use of coinage, although very few specimens of the gold daric of Darius I are still in existence, and each is now worth the equivalent of a camel load of gold in Darius' day. On them the king is shown running and carrying a bow, the symbol of authority. Herodotus tells us that young aristocrats were taught only three things at the Persian court: horsemanship, archery, and truthfulness.

Copies of the Bisutun inscription were evidently dispatched to every satrapy in the empire. Fragments of a papyrus from a Persian military settlement at Elephantine in Upper Egypt, now preserved in the Staatliche Museen in Berlin, bear portions of the Bisutun text translated into Aramaic. The chance discovery of these minor fragments is yet another indication of the extent of the Achaemenid Empire and the excellence of its administrative system.

Once the stonemasons and sculptors had completed their task at

Aramaic papyrus with the text of the Bisutun inscription

Gold coin of Darius I　　　　　　*Gold coin of Darius III*

Bisutun, the king ordered the steps leading up to the inscription to be destroyed. As a result, nobody could deface the stone document but nobody could read it either. It was almost as though Darius foresaw the advent, not only of Mohammed but also of modern archaeologists. Thanks to his prescience, the relief escaped the iconoclastic fury of fanatical Muslims and continued to adorn the rock face for twenty-five centuries, as mysterious as if it had been left there by a ghostly hand. When the script in which the text of the relief was carved had lapsed into oblivion, this inaccessible document in stone became a key to the deciphering of cuneiform. At the beginning of the modern era, European travellers studied the inscription through telescopes and made partial drawings of it. Grotefend, a professor from Göttingen, was the first man to decipher the king's name and title. Eventually, at considerable personal risk, a young East India Company officer named Rawlinson climbed the rock face and started to copy the inscription. Armed with mountaineering equipment, he made a second expedition to the site and resumed his copyist's activities by lowering himself down the cliff on a rope, an immensely laborious process. Later, when Rawlinson had succeeded in deciphering the cuneiform script, it was discovered that the inscription had been couched in three languages:

Impression of a cylinder seal. Darius the Great hunting lions

Median, Old Babylonian, and Old Persian, the latter was reserved for use in royal inscriptions.

The second gold coin depicts Alexander's adversary, Darius III, in the same posture and guise as Darius I. Artistic tradition had remained completely static, and no development had taken place in the intervening century and a half. The cylinder seal impression shows the Great King hunting lions, a royal sport to which Alexander was passionately addicted. The symbol above the chariot is that of Ahuramazda, the deity worshipped by the Achaemenids, but the difficult question of what religion the Persian kings professed is still unsolved. The inscription of the seal – here reproduced enlarged – is also trilingual, the languages being Persian, Elamite, and Babylonian.

Life at the Achaemenid court was both luxurious and fraught with danger. Within his own sphere of jurisdiction, each satrap lived like a petty king but whilst at court, he was exposed to the calumny and intrigue characteristic of struggles for power under any absolutist system. The king had only to grab a courtier by the belt in a fit of anger and the guards would march him out and strangle him. Such was the fate suffered by a Greek who gave Darius III some advice which, if followed, might have brought about Alexander's downfall.

Life at court was still further complicated by the sense of unease which habitually emanates from a harem guarded by eunuchs. It might be instructive to examine the career of one of the great satraps, a man about whom we know a great deal, including the nature of his personal appearance.

Tissaphernes (Persian: Cithrafarna) was satrap of Lydia and Caria as well as commander-in-chief of the Persian forces in Asia Minor. (Alexander, who had made a close study of Persian domestic politics, later separated the civil power from the military!) He lived at about the time of the Peloponnesian war. The unique coin bearing his portrait is particularly fine. To have minted it at all was an audacious act which clearly demonstrated the satrap's lordly attitude, for never before had the obverse of a coin been adorned with anything but a god, hero, or idealized monarch. This tetradrachm is not only the first coin to portray someone not of royal blood, but it is also the first

Two early silver coins struck by Persian satraps. Above, with the head of Tissaphernes; below, with that of Pharnabazus

to carry a genuine portrait of a human being. Greek sculptors had only just begun to make portrait busts in marble whilst Persian portraiture in marble was unknown. Tissaphernes was undoubtedly a grand seigneur and a man of high intelligence, nor was his autocratic cast of feature devoid of human appeal.

The satrap's misfortunes began when Darius II requested him to hand over tribute money from the Ionian cities of Asia Minor to the court treasury. Tissaphernes had already spent the money. To recoup, he dabbled in the intrigues between Sparta, Athens, the Persian court at Susa, and the Ionian cities, but without success. He incurred royal disfavour, was relieved of his military command in Lydia, and was succeeded by Cyrus the Younger, brother of Artaxerxes II. Tissaphernes quarrelled with Cyrus, who mustered an army on the pretext that he intended to fight the satrap but the army's true function was to depose Artaxerxes II. Tissaphernes first warned the king and then defeated Cyrus' army at Cunaxa, where Cyrus himself fell in battle. The satrap deprived the rebel prince's Greek mercenaries of their officers by means of a trick, but he could not prevent them from marching to the Black Sea coast under the command of Xenophon, a gentleman who had no previous military experience. Xenophon's *Anabasis*, which describes this epic march, provides us with a great deal of information about Asia Minor under Persian rule. It may also have given Alexander food for thought to learn that an army of Greek mercenaries could traverse such large areas of the Achaemenid Empire without let or hindrance. Tissaphernes eventually clashed with Pharnabazus, the satrap of Phrygia, who was just as much of a grand seigneur as himself and quite as arrogant, though not, perhaps, quite as congenial a character. Both men dabbled in the same world of intrigue. The only difference was that, when Tissaphernes came to Susa after his defeat and expulsion by Pharnabazus, all his past services to the throne could not save him from being executed at the insistence of the queen mother, who had never recovered from the death of Cyrus, her favourite son. As for Pharnabazus, whose disastrous failure to reorganize the Persian fleet went unpunished, he was given the hand of one of the king's daughters and entrusted with the reconquest of Egypt. Even though he failed yet again, he died in royal favour.

Such were the Persian grandees who in their youth learnt nothing but horsemanship, archery, and truthfulness. All of them fought bravely against Alexander in defence of their country. Having lost, some became the victor's loyal supporters while others continued to play the same old game of intrigue. Only a few fought to the bitter end.

Persepolis. Aerial photograph of the terrace

Athens. Aerial photograph of the Acropolis

Built on a man-made terrace in front of a rugged mountain back-drop, the royal seat of Persepolis presents a magnificent spectacle. Its splendour is comparable only with the beauty of the Athenian Acroplis, though the latter is older. The Acropolis was dedicated from mythical times onwards to the service of the gods, whereas Persepolis was the residence of an earthly ruler. The Parthenon was built later than Persepolis because the original temples on the Acropolis, which had been destroyed by Xerxes, were lavishly restored by Pericles. For all that, the splendour of the Achaemenid royal seat must have made an impression even on the supercilious Greeks. Only Alexander had no basis of comparison. He had never visited the Acropolis, never seen the Parthenon – never even been to Athens.

The beetling wall of rock known as Naksh-i-Rustam, part of which can be seen in the background on the extreme left of our picture, houses the tombs of the Achaemenid kings who lived at Persepolis.

Thousands of cubic yards of soil have been removed in the course of excavation, but the drawing by Daulier-Deslandes, dating from 1673, shows how much of Persepolis was still above ground in the seventeenth century.

The palace quadrangle adjoining the slopes is perceptibly darker than the rest of the site. This discoloration is a relic of the fire which destroyed the 'Hall of a Hundred Columns' after Persepolis had been

Persepolis. Seventeenth-century engraving of the ruins

94

captured by Alexander. The wall, built of massive ashlar blocks, is broken at one point by a double flight of broad, shallow steps. Climbing them, one involuntarily assumes an air of relaxed dignity. Even old Cornelius de Bruin, who ascended them in 1704, declared that their dimensions, which he recorded to the nearest inch, made them the most comfortable steps in the world. At the top the visitor is greeted by the 'Gate of Xerxes', here photographed from the interior. The approach road, which is miles long and absolutely straight, leads to Persepolis from the south. Visiting satraps had many hours in which to ponder their sins and misdemeanours within sight of their master's palace. The mountain which rises behind Persepolis was known as the Mount of Grace. The broad plain on the edge of which the royal residence stands is fertile land, and there was space enough in front of the palace for the king's entire army to parade in review order.

◀ *Persepolis. The Great Staircase*

Persepolis. The Gate of Xerxes

Persepolis. The Apadana, showing the eastern exit

Persepolis. Inscribed gold foundation tablet in its original stone case

Persepolis.
Griffin capital

The rigours of digging in dust and heat were nobly rewarded on the dramatic day when archaeologists unearthed a plaque covered with cuneiform characters. Made of solid gold and weighing over ten pounds, it has a beauty, majesty and intrinsic value which render it quite unique. The gold tablet bears particulars of the founding of Persepolis by Darius the Great, and was recovered undamaged from its original stone case. Europe had the opportunity to admire this superb piece when it was shown in an exhibition of Iranian art.

Although the builders of Persepolis relied chiefly on monumentality to convey the power of the Great Kings, they were not without a sense of harmony. The spacious quadrangles, though now littered with debris, are handsomely proportional to the halls and palace buildings. Particularly impressive are the numerous fallen capitals – massive monoliths which once supported wooden beams. The one illustrated above represents a griffin, but many of them take the form

97

Persepolis. Bodyguards at the eastern ascent to the Apadana ▶

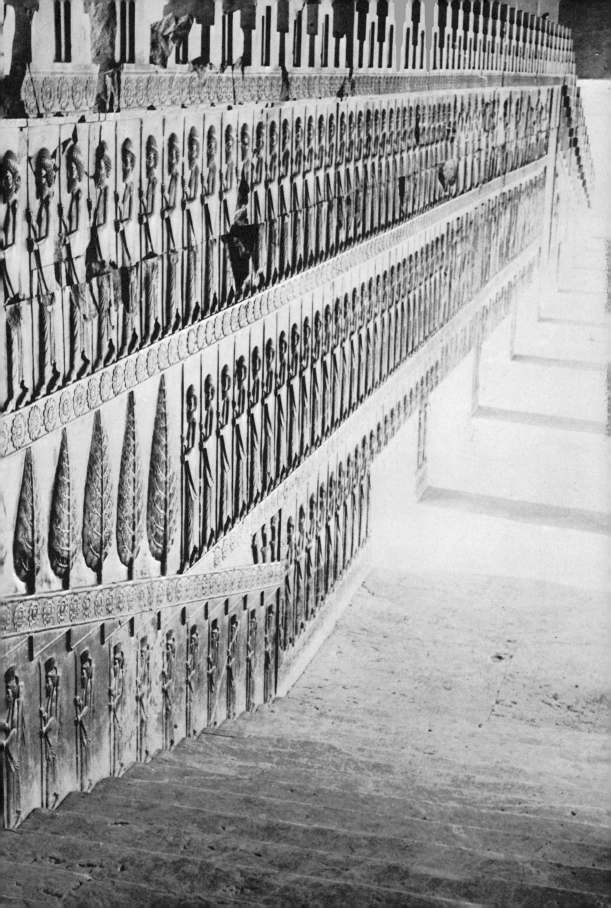

of bulls' heads. The columns were as much as 65 feet high, or almost twice as tall as the columns of the Parthenon. Thirteen columns of the Apadana or audience-chamber are still standing. One feat of architectural ingenuity which has long aroused admiration is the way in which the builders solved the problems posed by the lie of the land. The rocky bastion of Persepolis consists of three terraces of varying height and the walls of each terrace and the steps leading up to it are adorned with reliefs. Here, too, artistic treatment was mainly determined by a wish to convey the majesty of the King of Kings. For example, the long series of figures in one relief represents the annual procession which brought the monarch tribute transported by caravan from every corner of the empire. The treatment, though slightly monotonous, is far from schematic, and the facial differences between the various races are clearly brought out – the three bearded men in the section illustrated here are probably Syrians. By a quirk of fate, articles similar to those carried by the Syrians have actually been discovered. The gold bowl engraved with King Xerxes' name is preserved at Teheran, and the gold arm-band, which forms part of the so-called Oxus Treasure, is now in the British Museum. The silver amphora, from a private collection in Basle, bears a strong resemblance to the vessels carried by the leading member of the bearded trio.

Syrians bearing tribute in the form of vases, bowls and arm-bands. Some of the articles carried by the figures in this relief are still extant
Gold bowl engraved with the name of Xerxes. Gold arm-band from the Oxus Treasure. Silver amphora with handles in the shape of horses

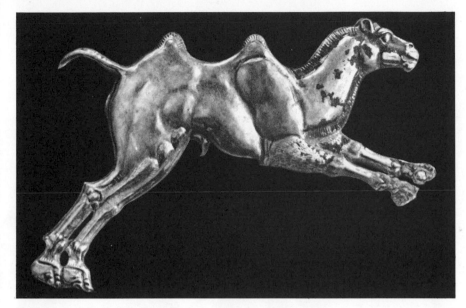

Gold figurine of a Bactrian camel

Gold ear-rings of the fifth–fourth century BC

There is a captivating elegance about some of the smaller Achaemenid works of art, e.g. the winged ibex in the Staatliche Museen in Berlin or the carved lapis lazuli head, probably of Xerxes, which was found at Persepolis (Colour Plate III). Also among the finest pieces are a gold rhyton (Colour Plate IV) and the bounding camel and gold ear-rings shown above.

The best-preserved building is the palace of Darius the Great, whose sombre diorite accentuates its air of austere solemnity. However, the palace also contained a small terraced flower-garden in which the ruler of the world could stroll when the mood took him.

◄ *Vase-handle in the shape of an ibex. Silver, partly gilded*

Persepolis. Palace of Darius the Great ►

Greek vase-painting. Darius the Great

Large reliefs occur mainly on the doorways. The tripylon seen here shows Darius seated on the throne with his son Xerxes standing behind him; a comparable scene exists on a fourth-century amphora in the Naples Museum. Viewed in conjunction, the two photographs show that the Greeks of Alexander's day cannot have been ignorant of the Achaemenid Empire – the Persian king's name, *ΔΑΡΕΙΟΣ*, is scratched into the paint above his head.

Persian sculpture sometimes attained heights of perfection. The dainty figure with a cloth over her left arm and an ointment bottle in her right hand possesses as much artistic merit as any Attic stele of the classical period. The sun of history no longer illumines the ancient splendours of Persepolis.

◄ *Persepolis. Relief of Darius the Great with his son Xerxes*

Persepolis. View from the terrace at sunset

Persepolis. A serving-woman in Darius' palace. Relief

Naksh-i-Rustam

The Great Kings were as exalted, stern and majestic in death as they were in life. At Naksh-i-Rustam, only an hour's ride from his palace, Darius discovered a rock face in the mountains and gave orders that his tomb should be hewn out of the cliff. Like the rock face at Bisutun, the tomb's frontage is adorned with reliefs and inscriptions. Other kings followed Darius' example, but their tombs now stand empty,

Rock face containing tombs of Achaemenid kings

only the inscriptions still speak of the great days of old. Half a millennium later, the Sassanian ruler King Shapur I had carved on the same wall his victory over the Roman emperors Philip the Arab and Valerian, as though – in Luschey's words – to inform the rulers of the past that Persia had regained her freedom and the glories of old had returned.

◄ *Naksh-i-Rustam. Tomb of Darius the Great*

Naksh-i-Rustam. Sassanid rock sculpture. Shapur I triumphing over the Roman emperors
Philip the Arab and Valerian

Naksh-i-Rustam. Sassanid rock sculpture showing investiture of Ardashir I.
Adjoining it on the right are the remains of an Elamite cult relief

There are many Sassanian rock sculptures in Iran, but they only occur in conjunction with Achaemenid sculptures at Naksh-i-Rustam. This same rock face bears traces of even older sculpture. Adjoining the investiture of King Ardashir I by Ahuramazda on the right is another Sassanian relief which partially covers an earlier Elamite work. Only one figure of this earlier cult relief which had adorned the rock face for over a thousand years when Darius installed his tomb there has survived. Darius' scribes could still read Elamite script – so can the scholars of the nuclear age.

Greek and Persian in hand-to-hand combat. Detail from a sarcophagus ▶
commissioned by King Abdalonymus of Sidon, known as the Alexander Sarcophagus

ALEXANDER'S CAMPAIGN against the Achaemenid Empire opened with the Macedonian army's crossing of the Hellespont in the spring of 334 BC. Alexander III, King of Macedonia, was twenty-two; Darius III, King of Kings and ruler of the largest empire in the known world, was forty-six. Having ascended the throne in the same year as Alexander, Darius had been obliged, like his future adversary, to restore internal order immediately after his accession. He then put down a rebellion in Egypt and, two years before Alexander, assumed the rank and title of Pharaoh in the ancient land bordering the Nile. Darius was anything but a weakling, neither was he without experience in military matters, though the society in which he had lived before his accession was not a warlike one despite its feudal structure. It was a world of luxury in art and life, a world of wealth and extravagance. The Persians had for generations pursued their political ends by diplomatic means. Minor military assignments were carried out by Greek mercenaries, of whom there was an adequate supply. Greece, with its steadily increasing population, suffered during these decades from a chronic food shortage which sometimes reached famine level. Even Alexander failed to eliminate these crises, so it was natural, if not entirely fair, that the Greeks should regard him and his campaign as the source of their economic ills. Domestic disputes within the Greek city-states, in which proscription was one of the commonest weapons employed, rendered many a leading figure homeless. Themistocles, the victor of Salamis, was exiled from Athens and sought refuge with the Persian king, who welcomed him in great style. Alexander's earliest successes against the Persians were achieved by defeating Greek mercenaries in the Persian service.

Alexander was obliged to recall the small army which King Philip had sent to Asia Minor during the last year of his reign to support the Ionian cities against the Persians. However, a small contingent had been left behind at the Hellespont by Parmenion, Philip's experienced general and comrade-in-arms. Consequently, the Macedonian army was able to make the crossing to Anatolia without harassment by the enemy. Alexander had crossed his Rubicon, the line dividing Europe from Asia. Running through the Aegean, the Hellespont, the Sea of Marmora, the Bosphorus and the Black Sea, this line of demarcation extended as far as the Caucasus. It had existed in the minds of the people of the Eastern Mediterranean since prehistoric times, just as it does today.

Alexander set foot on the soil of Asia at the very spot where Agamemnon had landed with the Achaean fleet, bent on conquering Troy. Only eight hundred years separated them, the same span which separates us from the Crusades, so it was hardly surprising that the king's thoughts turned to Homer. While aboard ship, he sacrificed to Poseidon, it being important to propitiate the ruler of the waves. From now on, the Macedonian army's supply line would be interrupted by water, and the enemy fleet was far superior to Alexander's. On landing, the king made sacrifice to the heroes who had fallen at the siege of Troy, starting with Achilles, the founder of his mother's line. He was courteous enough to make sacrifice to King Priam as well, for after the fall of Troy, Neoptolemus – the son of Achilles and thus another of Alexander's ancestors – had rather unheroically speared the elderly Trojan king to death at the altar of his palace.

There is no reason to pour scorn on the mythological reasons for the outbreak of this war. To call it a romantic escapade is to allow one's judgement to be clouded by latter-day condescension. Enlightened intellectuals of the fourth century BC regarded the myths with equal scepticism, but to soldiers they were as real as the clouds in the sky. Had not King Xerxes of Persia declared, when setting forth to conquer Hellas, that his aim was to avenge the destruction of Troy by the Achaeans?

Philip II's decision to give military aid to the Ionian cities had presented him with two problems. He had created a land-based power which counted for nothing on the sea and the only way of ensuring its permanency was to protect its long coast-line from naval attack. Although Philip had the requisite money and materials for ship-building, his Macedonian peasants were no seamen and the Greek sailors whom he could have recruited were not reliable enough. He decided to conquer Anatolia in the hope of expelling the Persian fleet from the Aegean by depriving it of its bases in Ionia. As his son was to discover later, Philip's calculations were not entirely accurate.

Apart from his military reasons for occupying the opposite shore of the Aegean, Philip had a psychological motive. In exercising sovereignty over Hellas, he had been shrewd enough to content himself with the status of 'captain-general' of the League of Corinth, which he had founded. Every major Greek city-state belonged to the League with the exception of Sparta, but Philip's wise policies had failed to compensate the Greeks for the joys of butchering each other. He hoped that a war conducted jointly by Greeks and Macedonians would endow his status as federal commander with a Panhellenic character.

Young as he was, Alexander adopted Philip's ideas, which were the fruits of a lifetime of political experience, and he weighed the odds dispassionately. His first act as king was to subdue the barbarians on his northern border. Marching southwards again at incredible speed to put down a revolt in Hellas, he learned that Demosthenes was contemptuously referring to him as 'boy Alexander' in the Agora. 'Well,' remarked the king, 'Demosthenes will find me grown into a youth by Thermopylae and a man by the time I reach Thebes.' In fact, Alexander was a man from the very first.

The mythological pomp which attended the crossing of the Hellespont not only fascinated the Macedonian army but emphasized the Panhellenic idea underlying the campaign. Nevertheless, Alexander's attempts to court sympathy among the Greeks met with little success. The farther he got from Europe the less inclined they were to follow him, until finally, when he had reached the foothills of the Hindu Kush, they launched a dangerous attack on his Macedonian base. His viceroy Antipater won a brilliant victory over Sparta, the main centre of Greek opposition. These troubles lay in the future, however. As with all wars, this one was still bathed in the radiance of its heroic beginnings.

The Persians did not interfere with the crossing of the Hellespont, even though it would have been easy enough for them to do so. They cannot have been unaware of the Macedonian army's march through Thrace, so their inaction may have been a product of overweening self-confidence. Alexander undoubtedly earned his successes, but his luck was so consistently good that it would be interesting to know what his horoscope looked like.

The Granicus, on whose banks the first battle was fought, rises on Mount Ida and flows into the Hellespont. The Persians had only mustered a relatively small force, and Alexander's army was numerically superior. The Persians made a number of tactical errors – Alexander, who made none, carried the day.

Since the military forces which the Persians maintained in this part of their empire were wiped out at the battle of the Granicus, Alexander was able to occupy Anatolia without undue exertion. Sardis, the ancient capital of Lydia, had become the seat of Persian power in Anatolia after the Lydians had been defeated but the city and all its treasures were surrendered without a struggle. Alexander took Mithrines, the satrap of Sardis, on to his staff and astonished his Macedonian grandees by treating the Persian aristocrat with exquisite courtesy. Later, when the women of the Persian royal family fell into his hands at Issus, he commissioned Mithrines to transmit a message of personal goodwill and inform them that Darius was still alive. The cities of Smyrna and Ephesus opened their gates to the 'liberator from the Persian yoke'. Miletus was taken after a brief struggle. Halicarnassus, the capital of Caria in the south-west corner of Anatolia, held out for some time but also fell to the Macedonians in the end.

Towards the end of this successful first year of war, Alexander took a picked band of alpine troops and set off on an expedition aimed at subduing Lycia, Pisidia and Pamphylia. Few soldiers who fought in the world wars of our own century could have been aware that they owed the rigours of winter warfare to Alexander the Great, for his military operations in South-West Anatolia, which lasted from autumn 334 until spring 333, were the first winter campaign in history. The mountain tribes in the inaccessible valleys of the Taurus Mountains had preserved a high degree of independence under the Persians and the object of Alexander's expedition was, as far as possible, to eliminate the risk of surprise attacks on his lines of communication. When spring came, the king rejoined the main body of his army, which had wintered at Gordium under the command of Parmenion.

Alexander might well have contented himself with the conquest of Anatolia, but it is evident that his plans went further than that from the outset. With surprising nonchalance, he completely disregarded the whole of the north and east of Asia Minor. Although this large and prosperous area could not have resisted seizure, he left it unconquered, nor did he remedy this omission subsequently. It is true that he appointed Mithrines satrap of Armenia some years later, but Mithrines seems to have been unable to take possession of the territory allotted to him. Orontes, the satrap appointed by Darius III, was still master of Armenia six years after Alexander's death.

Alexander's neglect of eastern Anatolia made itself felt in a quite unpredictable way. In Cappadocia, which was never incorporated in Alexander's empire, Greek and Persian culture met and mingled under conditions of freedom. A great-grandson of the last satrap appointed by Darius III had made himself king who, although Persian, was an enthusiastic philhellene, with the result that a lively and uninhibited exchange of ideas could take place under his aegis. This is one of the reasons why Cappadocia developed into a centre, not only of the Christian faith but also of Christian thought. The sponsors of this spiritual movement were the 'Cappadocian Fathers'. Christian theology, as Harnack once wrote, is a Gospel-based creation of Greek philosophy, and the Cappadocian Fathers were among its founders.

Alexander's omission was a remarkable risk to take. Had his opponent been Field-Marshal Kutusov, that great strategist would have lured him into the wide open spaces of Asia, and, while he was marching into the void, attacked him via Armenia and cut him off from his base. One of Darius' Greek advisers actually recommended such a course of action, but to the King of Kings this was an affront which cost the Greek his life. King Philip would have been put off by this strategic threat and contented himself with Anatolia, though he would, of course, have carefully consolidated his new dominions. It would have paid to extend Macedonia's sphere of influence to the Black Sea, with its numerous Greek coastal settlements; those on the northern coast provided a maritime outlet for the grain-lands between the Bug and the Don, as rich then as they are today. As a political structure, this enlarged Macedonia would have been extremely stable, it would, in fact, have occupied the sort of position which the Byzantine Empire successfully defended against attack from the East for centuries on end. Alexander's sights were set on higher things.

The Persians' military measures only confirmed Alexander in his determination to strike at the heart of Achaemenid sovereignty. Defeated on land, they proceeded to do what seemed to hold the best chance of swift success under prevailing circumstances: they attacked by sea. One Aegean island after another fell into their hands as, with alarming speed, they bore down on Alexander's most vulnerable spot, the Hellespont. Clearly, it had not been enough to oust the Persian fleet from its bases in Ionia because each base was permanently vulnerable to recapture from the sea. Alexander could neutralize the Persians' naval superiority only if he deprived them of every harbour in the Eastern Mediterranean. It was with this plan in mind that, in early summer 333 BC, he crossed the Taurus Mountains.

V   Darius III at the battle of Issus. Mosaic from Pompeii

Having occupied fertile Cilicia without encountering any resistance, he was struck down by a severe attack of fever. In the autumn of 333, barely recovered from his illness, he left Tarsus, the Cilician capital, and marched southwards along the Syrian coast. At Issus he was opposed by the Persian imperial army under the command of Darius himself. Darius was defeated, but Alexander did not pursue him although it was an age-old rule of war that a vanquished enemy should be pursued. Alexander resisted the temptation because his victories on land formed part of his maritime strategy. After weighing the odds with calculated precision, he stuck unflinchingly to his primary objective – to drive the Persians from the Mediterranean.

Alexander might have reached Egypt almost without drawing breath if it had not been for Tyre, the Venice of Phoenicia and mother-city of Carthage, which refused to open its gates to him. Hitherto considered impregnable, Tyre fell after seven months of siege and was totally destroyed. Gaza, too, had to be besieged and taken by storm before Alexander could occupy Egypt without meeting further resistance. He had attained his first major objective: the Persian fleet had ceased to exist. For the first and only time in history, a maritime power had been defeated by a land-based power.

Even Pericles had dreamed of uniting Hellas with Egypt. However, the Greeks did not thank Alexander for translating their greatest statesman's boldest idea into reality. The Eastern Mediterranean had been won for the Hellenic world, and the crowning glory of Alexander's military triumph was the founding of Alexandria in Egypt. Of the seventy-odd cities founded by him, only two were harbours, one at the mouth of the Nile and the other at the mouth of the Indus. From Egypt, sea-routes led to Ethiopia and India. What Alexander had in mind at the end of his eastern campaign was not the conquest of India but the opening of a sea-route to the Far East. Alexandria was destined to become the jewel of the Hellenistic world, a glittering scientific, artistic and commercial metropolis – to quote Droysen: 'the home and confluence of culture and literature from East and West'. Alexander left posterity no finer or more fitting memorial to his achievements.

From Memphis, the king made a pilgrimage to the oasis of Siwa in the Libyan Desert to question the oracle of Zeus Ammon. The high priest welcomed the new Pharaoh with deference and conducted him into the inner sanctum, but nobody has ever discovered the nature of the oracle's pronouncement. Whatever the son of Olympias learned about his divine descent in the desert shrine will for ever remain shrouded in obscurity.

VI   Alexander the Great at the battle of Issus. Mosaic from Pompeii

Bird's-eye view of the Dardanelles. ▶
Engraving by a French traveller of the seventeenth century

Constantinople

La Propontide ou Mer de Marm[a]

Gallipoli

Les Dardanelles

L'Hellespont

Chastean n[...]

Chasteau neuf d'Europe

Le Mont de Burse — Olympe Bitinie

Marmara

Golfe de Nicée

Le Simois

Le Xanthe ou Scamandre

de Troye

Cap Sigée

Before setting off once more for his distant objectives in the East, Alexander became a neighbour of Carthage by virtue of an alliance with Cyrene.

The Dardanelles, known in ancient times as the Hellespont, are roughly 45 miles long and well under a mile wide at their narrowest point. They link the Aegean with the Sea of Marmora. The artist's impression by Grelot, a French explorer who toured the East in the eighteenth century, is severely foreshortened but gives a good bird's-eye view of the geographical lay-out. The Bosphorus, which connects the Sea of Marmora with the Black Sea, begins at Constantinople.

To control the Dardanelles has always been a political objective of every sea-power in the Eastern Mediterranean. Even the Trojan War – with all due deference to the Muse of Poetry! – had a commercial background. The Trojans controlled all the sea traffic which used the straits, so the destruction of Troy gave the Achaeans free access to the Black Sea.

However colourful the legend of the Argonauts' voyage to Colchis, its underlying basis was an authentic journey of exploration with practical aims. The Argonauts were inspired by a wish to capture the Golden Fleece, and the Golden Fleece neatly symbolizes the wealth which accrued to Hellas over the centuries from the thriving lands adjacent to the Black Sea. Memories of the Argonauts' voyage lived on. Just as a would-be American aristocrat must boast an ancestor who crossed the Atlantic in the *Mayflower* in 1620, so, in Hellas, it was considered aristocratic to have a forebear who took part in the epic voyage of the *Argo*.

The Achaeans derived no benefit from their conquest of Troy. The Mycenaean civilization succumbed to invasion by the Dorian Greeks shortly after the Trojan War, but the Ionian cities of Asia Minor later founded numerous colonies on the shores of the Sea of Marmora and Black Sea. The Crimea became Greek, and Tanais, the easternmost settlement, lay as far afield as the estuary of the Don.

Many historic events have occurred in the vicinity of the Dardanelles. King Xerxes sent his army across the straits into Europe. Aegospotami, scene of the sea-battle in which Lysander decided the Peloponnesian War in favour of Sparta in 405 BC, was a city on the Thracian Cherso-nese, i.e. Gallipoli, the peninsula which juts far into the Aegean on the European side. The Emperor Constantine the Great planned to build the new eastern capital of the Roman Empire on the site of Troy and it is strange to reflect that if Constantine had not later decided to build his new Rome on the site of ancient Byzantium, at the entrance to the

Hissarlik, the hill that once was Troy

Bosphorus, Constantinople would now stand at the mouth of the Dardanelles.

The excavation of Troy marked the beginning of modern archaeology. To the layman, the hill of Hissarlik represents little more than an outsize rubbish-dump. Looking northwards from its summit, one

View of the Scamandrian Plain from Troy. In the background, Gallipoli

sees, running down to the water's edge, the 'Scamandrian Plain' on which the Trojans and Achaeans fought their battles. The range of hills on the horizon forms part of Gallipoli. The warriors of the Bronze Age were incapable of taking a fortified position by force of arms as siege techniques did not exist in the last quarter of the second millennium BC, so the fortress had to be taken by stratagem; ever since then, the Trojan horse – really an Achaean horse – has been one of the most popular metaphors in world literature.

The ruins of sacred Ilium were no longer in evidence when Alexander reached Troy, having sunk below ground-level long before. All Alexander found there was a wretched little Greek colonial town – christened Layer VIII by the American archaeologist Carl Blegen. Although it had been founded in 700 BC, long after the site had been abandoned, memories of the heroic battles of long ago lived on. In a temple dedicated to Athena, Alexander took down a shield reputed to have belonged to Achilles and hung his own on the wall in its place. The 'Shield of Achilles' may not have been the masterpiece, so brilliantly described by Homer, which Hephaestus forged in his divine smithy, however, Roman tourists still marvelled at Alexander's shield much as we do at the sword of Godfrey of Bouillon, which hangs in the Church of the Holy Sepulchre in Jerusalem.

Wild swans haunt the banks of the Granicus and a few cattle occasionally slake their thirst in its tranquil waters, yet this modest stream witnessed two momentous events. Paris sat beside its source on Mount Ida when deciding on the rival claims to beauty of the three goddesses, Hera, Athena, and Aphrodite. Wise as she was, even the Goddess of Wisdom would have liked to be the fairest of them, but it was Aphrodite, the Goddess of Love, not Athena, who won the golden apple. The other event stained the waters of the Granicus red. In the battle against the Macedonians, the Persians stationed their cavalry on an open slope on the right bank. Unwilling to let foreigners take the credit for victory, they left their Greek mercenaries in the background – this piece of arrogance and folly ensured their defeat. Granicus very nearly turned out to be Alexander's first defeat and last battle. Spithridates, satrap of Lydia and Ionia, supreme commander of the Persian army and son-in-law of the Great King, had already raised his battle-axe to cleave Alexander's skull when Cleitus, one of Philip's former comrades-in-arms, severed the Persian's arm from his body with one mighty sword-stroke.

*Silver coin of
Spithridates*

The Granicus, scene of Alexander's first battle against the Persians

Dascylium. Graeco-Persian relief of a mounted procession

Two archaeological treasures have been unearthed east of the Granicus at Dascylium, capital of the satrapy of Phrygia. One of the reliefs represents a mounted procession, the other a ritual sacrifice. Both works of art date from the middle of the fifth century BC and thus originated about a hundred years before Alexander's time. Western influence is hardly ever detectable in the Achaemenid sculpture of Susa and Persepolis, but both these reliefs display a rare and harmonious blend of Greek and Persian elements. Although their basic character is wholly Persian, the two sculptures clearly betray the influence of Greek art, both in their treatment of drapery and in their attempt to convey three-dimensionality by means of perspectival

Dascylium. Graeco-Persian relief of a sacrificial rite

devices – in other words, they brought a breath of Hellas into the official residence of an Oriental satrap. It is improbable that Alexander ever saw these reliefs. If he had, they would have proved to him that his projected fusion of Hellenic and Iranian culture was far from utopian.

Sardis was the capital of the powerful kingdom of Lydia between the eighth and sixth centuries BC. Archaeologists have excavated the Temple of Artemis there which was originally built by King Croesus in the sixth century, and was destroyed by the Athenians during the Ionian rebellion of 498 BC. Alexander gave orders that the Lydian's hallowed shrine should be restored.

Sardis. Temple of Artemis-Cybele ▶

Croesus was the last of the Lydian kings and a man whose name still symbolizes boundless wealth. He made lavish gifts to the oracular shrines at Delphi and Didyma, near Miletus, but Apollo rewarded him ill. When Croesus asked the Delphic oracle whether he ought to counter the growing menace of Persian strength by attacking first, he was told: 'If you cross the Halys you will destroy a great kingdom.' The Halys was the river separating Lydia and Persia. Croesus crossed it, but the kingdom he destroyed was his own. The Myson amphora depicts Croesus seated on a gorgeous throne on top of a pyre with his faithful servant Euthymus in the act of setting the logs ablaze. Legend has it that, after his defeat, Croesus resolved to atone for his presumption by sacrificing himself to the gods, but that Apollo saved him by sending a shower of rain. Like almost every story from Greek mythology, this one has several variants. According to another version, it was Cyrus who condemned his vanquished enemy to a fiery death. When the pyre was already alight, Croesus cried out: 'O Solon! O Solon!' Being inquisitive, like all intelligent people, Cyrus wondered what Solon of Athens had to do with the situation. He ordered the flames to be extinguished and asked Croesus what he meant. The defeated king told his conqueror about a visit he had received from Solon. Apparently, he had boasted of his wealth and power, but Solon's only response was to declare that no one should be deemed happy until his death. Solon's wise remark made Cyrus think twice. He pardoned Croesus and appointed him a member of his royal household where he continued to act as adviser to the Persian court under Cyrus' son Cambyses. This version of the story had the virtue of being edifying, so teachers from ancient times onwards used it for the instruction of boys who showed insufficient moral gravity.

Intelligent as he was, Alexander probably devoted little thought to Solon's sage dictum. He was too much the darling of the gods and too full of effervescent vitality. Sardis, which welcomed him so gaily that victorious spring, was the place where his ancestor Heracles had become involved in a torrid love affair with Queen Omphale of Lydia. It was also the city in which, fifteen years after Alexander's death, his only sister Cleopatra and her son were murdered – thus died the two surviving legitimate heirs to the Macedonian throne. The third had been Roxana's son Alexander.

Alexander's carefree days in Sardis were followed by a series of bitter political disappointments because the liberation of the Ionian cities led in many cases to bloody civil strife. The Persians had been shrewd enough to impose their authority on these troublesome Greeks

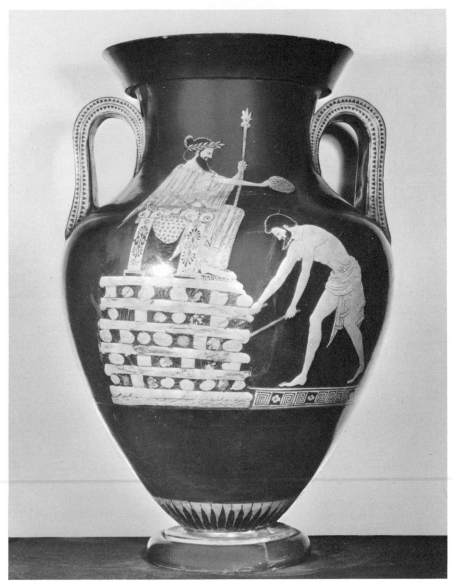

The Myson Amphora. King Croesus on his pyre

through the medium of other Greeks. Each city had a democratic party, which supported Alexander and the cause of liberation, and an oligarchy, which represented Persian interests. Even before the Macedonian army's arrival, the democrats of Ephesus rose in revolt against the oligarchs and embarked on a wholesale massacre which did not come to an end until Alexander appeared on the scene.

Ephesus.
Remains of the Artemision
with a Seljuk mosque and an
Ottoman castle in the background

Ephesus and Miletus were the two most important cities in Ionia at this time. They were also rivals. Miletus, situated at the mouth of the Maeander, had several good harbours but poor communications with the hinterland. Ephesus stood at the mouth of the Caÿster, which contained more mud than water and was constantly silting up the city's harbour. On the other hand, Ephesus was the terminal of the Persian royal highway which ran via Sardis to Susa. It also boasted the Artemision.

Legend has it that the famous Temple of Artemis was burnt down on the night of Alexander's birth. Reconstruction had already started, and Alexander decreed that the tribute money formerly paid by the

Ephesians to the Persians should now be given to the priesthood of Artemis. The Artemision was one of the Seven Wonders of the Ancient World, both before and after the fire. It took years to find the original site, which seems hardly surprising when one looks at the excavated fragments of marble which are all that remain of one of the ancient world's most magnificent buildings. On the hill in the background stands an Ottoman castle, in the centre of which is a ruined basilica housing the tomb of St John. The building with the two pointed gables at the foot of the castle is a mosque, a masterpiece of Seljuk architecture, built in wonderful reddish marble taken from the Artemision.

Ephesus. The Artemision, reconstructed by Fischer von Erlach

In 1721, the great baroque architect Fischer von Erlach attempted to reconstruct the famous building from the ancient descriptions. He also made use of a Roman coin bearing a symbolic representation of the Artemision, here seen in the top left corner of his drawing, which provided him with a reference for the central portion of the temple frontage. Fischer von Erlach's reconstruction does not differ substantially from those made by modern archaeologists, except that no one realized at the beginning of the eighteenth century that the Artemision stood beside the water, its foundations forming part of the harbour wall.

VII   Alexander the Great in battle. Detail from a relief on one side of the Alexander Sarcophagus

Ephesus. Silver coin representing the Artemision

Viewed in conjunction, the fragmentary column from the Artemision and the statue of Artemis give an idea of the tensions that existed in an area in which the spirit of Greece had for centuries been subjected to Asian influence. Not only did Alexander see the original statue, but there can be little doubt that he examined it closely. Our illustration of the column shows Alcestis, who has descended into Hades in place of her husband Admetus, being turned away by Persephone. It is one

VIII   Hunting panther.
Detail from a relief on one end of the Alexander Sarcophagus

Ephesus. Base of a column from the Artemision

Ephesus. Marble effigy of Cybele-Artemis

of the thousand stories from the flourishing garden of Greek mythology, distinguished from others only by the fact that Euripides based
one of his tragedies on it. The goddess, a Roman copy in wonderful
Parian marble, betrays no trace of Greek influence. Her elaborate
symbolic finery is still that of the ancient Asiatic mother-goddess
Cybele. The Artemis of Ephesus was revered by Greeks and Orientals
alike, but one can well imagine what an abomination this effigy must
have seemed to St Paul – himself the harbinger of a religion which
hailed from the East.

A brilliant future lay in store for Ephesus. The city played an important role in the Hellenistic era, under the Roman Empire, and again in the early centuries of Christendom. The magnificent arcade which led from the theatre to the harbour was paved with marble and illuminated by night, shops nestled beneath the arches on either side, as they do in every oriental bazaar to this day.

Priene, situated on the southern slopes of Mycale, stands on a series of terraces ranging from one hundred to over four hundred feet above the plain. In the north, a spur of solid marble soars to a height of nearly one thousand feet. At its summit stands the city's acropolis. To sit down on the slight slope in the shade of the Aleppo pines is to take a ring-side seat in the arena of history and gaze far into time and space. To the east, veiled in blue haze, the jagged peaks of the Latmus Mountains jut into the radiant sky; south, at the foot of the range of hills opposite lies Miletus; west, there is a prospect of open sea with the island of Samos gleaming on the horizon. The river in the plain is the Maeander, so serpentine and convoluted that it gave its name to one of the most popular ornamental motifs in Greek art.

Priene. View of the Maeander Valley ▶

Miletus. Wall of the Roman amphitheatre

Priene and Miletus were once separated by open water, rivers can move mountains, however, and the bay became silted up in the course of centuries. There is not a town on this luminous coast, large or small, which does not have an important tale to tell. In the middle of the sixth century BC, Priene was the home of Bias, one of the Seven Sages. The threat presented by the growing power of Persia prompted him to summon the inhabitants of the Ionian cities to abandon the western coast of Asia Minor and jointly found a new city in Sardinia. Had this suggestion been adopted, the Western Mediterranean might also have become Hellenized. Another man who grew up in Priene's narrow streets was Hermogenes, one of the architects of Hellenism. His writings, which Vitruvius drew on in the work he dedicated to the Emperor Augustus, continued to influence architects until the Renaissance. It might be said that the dismembered columns at Priene are the ancestors of the columns in St Peter's at Rome.

Miletus was the city of the dawn, the place where the classical civilization of Greece really began. Here lived Thales, another of the Seven Sages and a pioneer in the study of natural phenomena. Thales was the great mathematician and astronomer who predicted the solar eclipse of 28 May, 585. Miletus was the first Greek city to mint coins, produce maps of the known world, and publish manuals of seamanship. Its inhabitants retained a certain measure of independence by concluding a treaty with Cyrus the Great at an early stage.

Almost every one of the islands off the Ionian coast is associated with some famous name or other. Sappho lived on Lesbos, Homer on Chios, Pythagoras on Samos, Hippocrates on Cos. Ionia also played an important role in the history of Christianity. St John received his revelation on Patmos and two Church councils were held at Ephesus. The Latmic Gulf witnessed several major incidents in the struggle between the Greeks and Persians. In 496/495 BC the Ionians were defeated by the Persians at the sea-battle of Lade. Then a small island off Miletus, Lade has since become a hill projecting from the alluvial plain. In 479, one year after the battle of Salamis, the Spartan king Leotychidas won a great victory over the Persians at Mycale, but not even this secured Ionia's freedom for long. Later, the citizens of Priene had a grandstand view of the hostilities between Alexander and the Persians. Alexander's handful of ships had managed to reach the Latmic Gulf before the powerful Persian fleet and seize one of the harbours of Miletus. The walled city resisted Alexander stoutly and was attacked from the landward side. The Persian fleet dropped anchor off Priene and sailed past Miletus in battle order each morning, daring Alexander to come out and fight. The king, however, was doubly unwilling to risk defeat because not even victory would have availed him much. The Persians had reserves, unlike him, so one naval success would not have gained him mastery of the sea. The cat-and-mouse game continued for some days until Alexander sent soldiers to the Persians' anchorage to prevent enemy seamen from landing and fetching water. Then, one day, the whole of the Persian fleet sailed away to Samos. It was probably the only time in history that infantrymen had compelled an entire fleet to abandon a maritime position. Miletus was taken after a brief struggle.

Alexander's experience with the Persian fleet in the Latmic Gulf prompted him to adopt a startlingly logical course of action. Since his own fleet was too small to force a decision, he simply disbanded it and enrolled the ships' crews in his army. This decision gave the enemy a completely free hand on the sea, and Memnon of Rhodes, who commanded the Persian fleet, was a dangerous man. He started to reconquer the Aegean island by island, banking on the likelihood that if he cut off Alexander entirely from mainland Greece the Greeks would rise in revolt against the Macedonians. This menacing situation resolved itself in an unexpected way. Memnon died, and Darius deprived his successor Pharnabazus of the one tool which the admiral would have needed in order to consolidate the conquests made by the fleet. To reinforce his already enormous imperial army still further, Darius ordered that the Greek mercenaries doing marine duty aboard Persian ships should be put ashore and marched off to join him.

ALEXANDRI FORTUNA – Alexander's luck – aroused such amazement, even in the ancient world, that Plutarch devoted an entire essay to the subject.

Nothing has survived of the Miletus of Alexander's day. The Roman market gate was excavated by Wiegand and is now preserved in Berlin, thanks to the cordial relations which prevailed between the Kaiser and Sultan Abdul Hamid of Turkey. The wall, composed of fine ashlar blocks bearing scenes from a boar-hunt, belongs to a later amphitheatre, also Roman. By contrast, the Heraeum or temple dedicated to the goddess Hera on Samos dates from archaic times. Erected shortly after the downfall of the tyrant Polycrates, the venerable shrine subsided into the marshy ground and was not unearthed until our own day.

A day's march south of Miletus stands the Temple of Apollo at Didyma. The oracle of Didyma enjoyed so wide a reputation in the ancient world that powerful rulers such as Pharaoh Necho of Egypt

Didyma. Marble lion with columns of the Temple of Apollo in the background

and King Croesus of Lydia sent votive gifts to the temple. Didyma was looted by the Persians early in the fifth century and Canachus' famous bronze statue of Apollo carried off to Iran. The oracle fell silent. Under Alexander's aegis it gave voice once more, prophesying great things in store for the Macedonian king. The statue of Apollo, which Seleucus I later restored to the temple, often appeared on the coins of Miletus and, subsequently, of other places.

The head of Medusa comes from the temple frieze and the huge lion, which dates from the middle of the sixth century, probably stood guard over a grave. All these early sculptors are anonymous.

Two coins representing the Canachus Apollo

Didyma. Head of Medusa from the frieze in the Temple of Apollo

148

The Taurus Mountains in early winter

The fighting at Halicarnassus, though destined to drag on for a considerable time, completed the conquest of the Ionian coast.

Alexander sent all his young married soldiers on leave – another measure with a very modern flavour. He dispatched Parmenion to the interior of Anatolia with the cavalry, engineers and baggage train, designating Gordium as the headquarters of this part of the army. Then he embarked on his winter campaign in Pamphylia, Lycia and Pisidia, choosing winter for his attack on the mountain tribes in these remote areas because they would be concentrated in the valleys and unable to escape to higher ground because of snow.

The south coast of Anatolia is reminiscent of the Riviera, except that there is no continuous road, outlying spurs of the Taurus run southwards to the sea, repeatedly punctuating the coastline with steep cliffs. As a result, anyone traversing the country in an easterly direction and wishing to get from one valley to the next finds himself compelled, again and again, to strike inland and make for one of the passes high in the mountains. Apart from being fertile and well watered, the

View of the south coast of Anatolia ▶

countryside possesses great scenic beauty. At one place, the cliff of Chelidonia, continuous northerly winds can cause the water to recede far enough to allow a sizeable body of men to march along the foot of the cliff. As soon as the wind shifts, the path is swallowed up again by the sea. The north wind had been blowing for several days when Alexander reached the cliff, so his men skirted it dry-shod. The wind backed immediately afterwards, engulfing the path they had just used. The unsophisticated Macedonian soldiers naturally construed this as direct intervention by the gods in favour of their adored, admired and incomparable king.

When spring came, Alexander and his small force of alpine troops rejoined the main body of the army.

Gordium, the ancient capital of Phrygia, reached its zenith in the eighth century BC. Alexander had selected the city as the army's winter quarters because it dominated the road from Troy to the Cilician Gates and another point in its favour, it stood beside a river, the Sangarius, whose lush water-meadows would provide grazing for the horses in the spring, as well as the fodder so essential to any further advance.

Pamphylia. The Manavgat Falls   *The cliff of Chelidonia* ▶

The Macedonian troops must have derived great pleasure from Anatolia, with its host of myths, tales and legends. Long before, a peasant named Gordius had been driving his ox-cart to Telemessus, a town in the west of the Taurus, when an eagle perched on the shaft of his wagon. It was enough that Gordius had received this sign from Zeus for him to be proclaimed successor to the king, who had just died, as soon as he entered Telemessus. Many a soldier must have cast an occasional glance at the sky in the hope that one of the eagles circling above would settle on his shoulder and give his military career a welcome fillip. Gordius dedicated a temple to his ox-cart in the city of Gordium, which he later founded. The shaft of the cart was attached to the yoke by means of a knotted bark cord. According to an oracle, the man who succeeded in untying this knot was destined to become master of Asia. The story that Alexander cut the famous Gordian Knot with his sword corresponds so well with the superficial notion that he was a man of violence that it is doubtful if the legend will ever die. All we know, thanks to painstaking research, is that the incident never occurred at all – the conquest of a continent was not to be bought as cheaply as that. Much of Gordium has been excavated and a small section of the Persian royal road unearthed at the entrance to the city. The road, which was about eighty feet wide, had a firm, smooth, metalled surface.

Gordium. View of the excavations

Alexander remained at Gordium until July, waiting for things to mature in the Aegean. Whatever happened, Gordium was near enough to enable him to get back to Greece quickly in an emergency. As soon as the threat had passed, he continued his advance.

The Taurus Mountains, which possess only one really serviceable pass, the Cilician Gates, would have provided Syria and Mesopotamia with a massive natural rampart. Easy as it would have been for the Persians to defend the pass, however, they neglected to do so. At one point, in a gorge enclosed by smooth walls of rock, the road consisted only of a timber gallery supported on beams driven into the rock itself; the destruction of this gallery would have blocked the gorge. Today, the road runs past on the other side of the gorge and the holes for the wooden supports can still be seen. As it was, Alexander negotiated the awkward defile without meeting any resistance and reached Tarsus, the capital of Cilicia. Having caught a severe fever there and been cured by his skilful physician, Philippus of Acarnania, he was compelled to remain in Tarsus by an unexpected development.

The Cilician Gates

Tarsus. English lithograph of the nineteenth century

Like the cities of Ionia, Tarsus played an important role once Hellenism had become a power in the world. Cicero was the Roman governor of Cilicia, and tradition has it that he administered the province admirably. Tarsus was the scene of Antony's first meeting with Cleopatra, boarding her gilded barge with its awning of royal purple, the Egyptian queen had herself rowed up the river while Antony sat alone in the agora. The entire population had flocked to the water's edge, anxious not to miss the spectacle of a queen reclining on her bed of state in the guise of Aphrodite. Tarsus was also the birthplace of St Paul and the burial place of Julian the Apostate, the last heathen to occupy the throne of imperial Rome.

The battlefield of Issus lies between the sea and the Amanus Mountains, which separate Syria from the coast. The strip of land between the shore and the low hills in the background is two and a half miles wide and the aqueduct dates from Roman times. This bleak plain, bare of anything save scrub, was the scene of a battle which shaped the course of world history for centuries to come – indeed, the effects of Alexander's victory can still be felt in our own day. Battle was joined as a result of tactical errors on both sides, errors which led to grotesque confusion. Alexander, who had marched straight past the Persians, suddenly found them behind him. He turned his entire army about and attacked in a northerly direction. The outcome of the battle was decided by the low range of hills in the background. The impenetrable undergrowth covering the slopes hampered Darius' freedom of movement so greatly that he was unable to exploit his numerical superiority. The crucial moment of the battle is depicted in a mosaic found at Pompeii (Colour Plates V and VI). Equally graphic is the scene on a vase from southern Italy, which shows Alexander and Darius locked in mortal combat. If the incident on the vase had actually occurred, Darius would never have survived. The two kings may not even have got as close as the Pompeii mosaic suggests, yet it does convey the essentials: Alexander's grim determination, and, in the case of his adversary, a hesitation, uncertainty and bewilderment which ultimately turned into panic and dismay. The painter depicts the peripeteia, or crucial moment when Darius realizes that he has lost the day and decides to flee.

'Neither our own age nor posterity,' Goethe wrote a few days before his death, 'will ever succeed in commenting adequately on such a miracle, and we are repeatedly compelled, after close scrutiny and investigation, to resort to plain and unadulterated wonderment.'

Preserved for us by the eruption of Vesuvius, the mosaic is based on a major contemporary painting by Philoxenus. Since none of the masterpieces of Greek fourth-century painting – which the Greeks prized more highly than sculpture – has survived, we have every reason to be delighted with the Issus mosaic. The problems of the art historian can be gauged from a work published by Heydemann in 1883, in which he pointed out that the 'battle of Issus' interpretation was only one of eighteen different interpretations known to him.

The Persians sustained very heavy casualties, more of them during the pursuit than in the battle itself – the Persian royal army had been destroyed – Darius and a handful of loyal soldiers fled through Syria and across the Euphrates to Babylon. Alexander steadfastly refused

Issus. The battlefield

South Italian vase-painting. Alexander and Darius in battle

Pompeii. Mosaic of the battle of Issus

either to pursue his beaten adversary or to linger over the spoils of war. He merely sent Parmenion with a small detachment to Damascus, which had been Darius' headquarters, with orders to safeguard all plunder.

Damascus is an oasis in the southern spurs of the Anti-Lebanon. Seen from the air today, the splendid palm-fringed city still looks much as it does in the bird's-eye impression below, which was drawn by a Dutch traveller of the seventeenth century. It yielded vast quantities of booty comparable only with the treasures acquired by the Goths in Rome, the Crusaders in Constantinople, and the Mongols in Peking. Susa, Persepolis and Pasargadae yielded further mountains of gold, plate, purple cloth, and ivory, but the plunder from Damascus was enough in itself to dispel any worries Alexander may have entertained about the further financing of his campaign. Among other spoils from the Persian royal household, Parmenion notified Alexander of the following:

Damascus. Dutch engraving of the seventeenth century

Cedars of Lebanon

329 female musicians and singers
 46 garland-weavers
277 kitchen-hands
 29 chefs
 40 unguent-mixers
 70 wine-warmers

Alexander was surprized to find that Damascus harboured envoys accredited to the Persian court by Athens, Thebes and Sparta, and nothing could have been more typical of his political acumen than the way in which he dealt with these awkward problems. The Thebans he released without more ado, since their hostility was understandable in view of the Macedonians' destruction of their city. The Athenians he sent home as though a spot of treachery behind their captain-general's back were a mere bagatelle. We may be sure that the haughty Athenians were more than a little disconcerted by such treatment. As for the Spartans, with whose country he was virtually at war, Alexander respected their diplomatic immunity in accordance with ancient and hallowed tradition. He first arrested the Spartan ambassador and then released him, possibly so that he could spread word of the Macedonian successes.

Alexander marched rapidly southwards, following the coastline. The weather was temperate at this season and the army's route took it through some extremely beautiful country; on the right lay the glistening blue sea, on the left the cedar-clad slopes of the Lebanon. Solomon had used this precious wood for the adornment of the Temple in Jerusalem, the Pharaohs had used it to build the Egyptian ships which circumnavigated Africa, and cedar wood still travels the seas today under the Lebanese flag. Isolated clumps in the high and inaccessible valleys of the Lebanon are all that remain of these magnificent trees, and proper cedar forests survive only in the Taurus and Atlas.

The Alexander Sarcophagus, found at Sidon

At Sidon Alexander deposed King Straton, distrusting his undue eagerness to collaborate, and, leaving the choice of a successor to Hephaestion, he continued his march. Hephaestion discovered a distant scion of the royal house named Abdalonymus working as a humble gardener in one of the suburbs who, since he was a man of unblemished character, Hephaestion installed as the new ruler of Sidon. Gratitude is a rare virtue, but Abdalonymus commissioned a marble sarcophagus which still extols the fame of his benefactor to this day. Discovered in a vault at Sidon, it is miraculously well-preserved. One side of the sarcophagus represents Alexander at the battle of Issus and the other shows him conducting a lion hunt with a party of Persian guests, and therefore, because of these reliefs, it is known as the Alexander Sarcophagus. One of the finest early Hellenistic

165

works of art in existence (Colour Plates VII, VIII), it is now a prized possession of the Archaeological Museum in Istanbul.

Acting in concert, the Phoenician coastal cities could have given Alexander a great deal of trouble, especially if they had managed to secure aid from Carthage. The Phoenicians, however, had little reason to oppose him, Phoenicia and Syria had always been a bone of contention between Egypt and the successive empires of Mesopotamia and Persian sovereignty had now collapsed. The Phoenicians could not hope for complete independence so they yielded to the Macedonians, hoping to offset the temporary loss of their markets in the East by trading with Hellas.

The problems which might have been posed by concerted resistance on the part of the Phoenician cities can be deduced from the trouble Alexander had with Tyre. It took him seven months of immensely arduous siege warfare to capture the city. The Tyrians felt very sure of themselves, or they would never have gambled on resistance – Nebuchadnezzar had besieged their city in vain for thirteen years. Alexander did not succeed until he had mustered a new fleet and used it to blockade the enemy ships in their harbours, the city was then totally destroyed and most of its inhabitants butchered. Having captured Tyre and Gaza, which had also put up a fight, Alexander entered Egypt at the head of his army in December 332 BC.

166

Tyre. Fallen columns on the shore ▶

*Luxor. Alexander presenting
offerings to Ammon-Min*

To the Egyptians, the Macedonian
king was the man who had come
to free them from the hated Persian
yoke and Alexander behaved with
the utmost tact. He won over the
priesthood by sacrificing to the
sacred bull in the temple of Ptah
at Memphis, the intelligentsia by
holding games and artistic contests,
and the peasantry by overhauling
the system of government and
taxation. A carved relief in the
temple at Luxor shows him presenting offerings to the god Ammon-Min, proving that the priesthood readily acknowledged him to
be the new Pharaoh.

Memphis. Temple of Ptah   169

Aerial view of modern Alexandria

Alexander crowned his conquest of the Eastern Mediterranean by founding Alexandria, the first of some seventy cities to be built at his behest. The outlines of Alexandria and its network of roads were marked out in the sand on a tongue of land between the sea and a reed-filled lake and the city built according to a unified plan from the outset. The Greeks of the fourth century BC were far in advance of our own chaotic urban developers.

The Egyptians were not unduly delighted with Alexander's new foundation because they did not like foreigners. It was true that merchants from Miletus had obtained permission to found a Greek city in the Nile Delta around the middle of the seventh century.

170

Alexandria. Personification of the city

However, their city, Naucratis, was rather like nineteenth-century
Shanghai, whose autonomy the Chinese guaranteed because they
considered Europeans to be unworthy of their emperor's sage
jurisdiction.

Although situated on the Mediterranean coast, Alexandria was linked
with the Red Sea by the Nile and a canal and became the largest port
in the Mediterranean within a few decades. The figure in the mosaic
picture dating from the first half of the third century BC is a martial
personification of Alexandria. The head-dress takes the form of a ship
and the staff with the crosspiece symbolizes a ship's mast. The inscription in the top left corner is the artist's signature.

Bronze coin of the Emperor Antoninus Pius. The Pharos of Alexandria

When Napoleon landed in Egypt, Iskenderia-Alexandria was a township of five thousand inhabitants. Today, it is once more an international port. On a small off-shore island, linked with the mainland by a mole, stood a lighthouse which was one of the Seven Wonders of the Ancient World. Built between 299 and 279 BC, it was 360 feet high and remained standing until AD 1326. The Pharos, which is still commemorated by the French word for lighthouse, was much favoured by the artists of antiquity. We here see it used as the reverse type of a coin struck under the Emperor Antoninus Pius in the first half of the second century AD. Colour Plate XI shows it depicted on a glass vase unearthed at Begram in Afghanistan.

Marble head of King Ptolemy I Soter ▶

Alexandria. Khait Bey fort, the former island site of the Pharos

It was the Ptolemaic dynasty which made Alexandria the capital of
Hellenism. The kings supplemented wealth acquired through trade
with the luxuries of education, art, and scientific research. The first
of this royal line, Ptolemy I Soter, was one of Alexander's generals.
The last member of the brilliant family of Macedonian aristocrats
which had ruled Egypt for almost three centuries was Cleopatra VII.
The age of Hellenism, inaugurated by Alexander the Great, came to
an end with her. After Cleopatra's death Egypt degenerated into a
province of the Roman Empire.

Before Alexander embarked on any new ventures he made a pilgrimage
to the oasis of Siwa. The French explorer Jomard included an admirably clear sketch of the oasis in his *Voyage à l'Oasis de Syouah*, which
appeared in 1823. Siwa was an island of bustling life in a vast sea of
desert. Vestiges of the temple of Zeus Ammon, into which the high
priest once conducted Alexander, can be seen to this day.

Oasis of Siwa. Nineteenth-century engraving

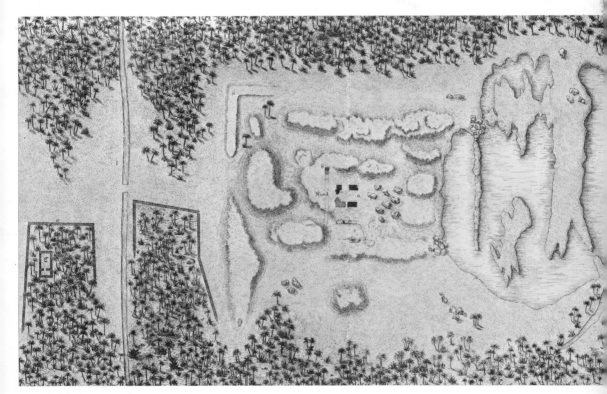

◄ *Silver coin of King Ptolemy I Soter*

Oasis of Siwa. Temple of Zeus Ammon

Graeco-Aramaic inscription of King Asoka, discovered near Kandahar in Afghanistan. Third century BC

IV Victory without End

THE OCCUPATION OF EGYPT placed Alexander the Great in an extremely odd strategic position. The primary object of his attack on the Achaemenid Empire, the neutralization of Persian sea-power, had been accomplished. Alexander now possessed an effective fleet of his own. Although this fleet guaranteed him control of the Aegean and secured his supply line across the Hellespont, it was no use to him in his further operations against Darius. There was no power left in the Eastern Mediterranean against which it could have been employed, and the only maritime power in the Western Mediterranean was Carthage with whom Alexander maintained good diplomatic relations. Pursuing a policy of caution reminiscent of Venice in later times, the Carthaginians had remained aloof from the warlike developments in the Eastern Mediterranean, even though intervention by their fleet could have prolonged the Macedonian siege of Tyre indefinitely. The Carthaginian sphere of influence was the Western Mediterranean whence her ships skirted the shores of the Atlantic bound for England and, possibly, even at this period, Norway to the north, the Cameroons in the south. Carthaginian envoys had fallen into Alexander's hands when Tyre fell, but he treated them with the utmost courtesy and sent them home without imposing conditions of any kind. This might have intimated that he had no designs on the powerful Phoenician city, but it might equally have signified that he did not intend to take action against it for the time being. We do not know whether or not Alexander regarded the occupation of the North African coast as a worthwhile objective; every conqueror of Egypt has been beguiled by the prospect of advancing along the narrow and, at that time, fertile strip of land between the Nile Delta and the Pillars of Hercules – today the Straits of Gibraltar. Success would have meant control of the entire Mediterranean, which must undoubtedly have seemed larger to the contemporary world than the Atlantic does to us today.

The Carthaginians had already undergone some disquieting experiences with past conquerors of Egypt. Cambyses, son of Cyrus the Great, launched an attack on them from the Nile Valley but was foiled when his army perished in a sandstorm. Unable to resist a similar temptation, the Arabs of our own era got as far as Southern France via Gibraltar and Spain.

One question which recurs constantly is whether Alexander was a conqueror and nothing more. Since he conquered more territory than any general before or after him, it seems natural to suppose that conquest was his aim in life, but that assumption does not do justice to Alexander the statesman. To him, power was always a means to something greater. Even when he had bent the East to his will, he did not turn against the West. Instead, he fitted out an expedition – one of the largest ever mounted – to explore the sea-route from the Persian Gulf to the Red Sea, planning to turn it into a safe and permanent shipping lane. The Carthaginians could foresee none of this, but they very soon learned that they had been granted a respite. Hamilcar, a senior Carthaginian army officer whom Alexander had taken on to his staff, acted as their spy in the Macedonian headquarters, and he informed them that operations against the Achaemenid Empire were to continue. Darius had communicated with Alexander by letter soon after the battle of Issus. Writing as 'King of Kings', he demanded the release of his captive family. The very fact that Darius put the young Macedonian ruler on a plane with himself, the Great King, was not only remarkable but indicative of the Persian's realism and common sense. The younger monarch rejected the elder's demands. The concluding words of Alexander's letter to his adversary, an interesting personal document, read as follows:

'Since I am now lord of all Asia, come to me. But, if you have any fears on this score, send some of your friends, that they may receive sureties. Ask in person for your mother, your wife, your children, and whatsoever else you desire to ask, and you shall receive it, for whatsoever I deem just you shall have. Furthermore, when you send me word, send to the King of Asia and do not write as though to an equal, but, if you request something, address yourself to the master of all that was yours. Otherwise, I shall exact vengeance. But, if you still wish to contend for sovereignty, give battle and do not flee, for I shall seek you everywhere.'

The letter is a singular mixture of magnanimity, braggadocio and quite incredible exaggeration. The braggadocio may have been feigned, since Alexander must have been fully alive to the weaknesses of his position. The magnanimity was genuine, but there could be no talk of Alexander's mastery of Asia. The Persians had lost one major battle and a number of countries on the fringe of their empire. Their real seat of power, High Iran, was completely intact, Alexander had not even secured Mesopotamia, which adjoined the Iranian highlands in the west. How far he was from being 'Lord of Asia' at this stage can be gauged from the trials he had to undergo before he became so.

After his first proposal had been rejected, Darius made another approach to his haughty and inexorable foe. This time, Darius' terms were surprisingly generous. He offered Alexander ten thousand talents in gold, the hand of his daughter, and a dowry consisting of all the territory west of the Euphrates. Coming, as it did, from a man who was still undefeated, this peace offer was unique in its generosity. The choice of the Euphrates as a frontier bore witness to the Persian king's political discernment. Darius evidently knew something about international relations. No oriental power has ever succeeded in consolidating its hold on conquered territory west of the Euphrates, just as no European power has ever managed to assert its authority permanently to the east of that river.

There is an anecdote about the discussions that went on at Alexander's headquarters over Darius' peace terms. When asked for his opinion, Parmenion is said to have replied that, if he were Alexander, he would accept Darius' proposal, whereupon the king observed that, were he Parmenion, he would do the same. The antithesis is too contrived to carry the ring of truth. Alexander may have suffered from occasional fits of arrogance, but he was not foolishly conceited. It would have been out of keeping with his innate nobility of character to make such a gratuitously insulting remark to an old and respected general. In this instance, the kernel of truth is buried very deep. Alexander had some brilliant achievements to his credit, but so had King Philip. That which was to surpass the bounds of normality still lay in the future. Nobody could have said at this stage that Alexander had earned a higher status than his father. It therefore seems likely that Parmenion, whose entire career had been linked with Philip's successes, would have expressed himself in favour of accepting the Persian offer. He may even have opined that King Philip would have accepted Darius' terms, and Alexander may have replied that, in King Philip's place, he would have done the same. Alexander could not have meant to condescend to his chief of staff. It is more probable that he wanted to free himself from the father-figure which had dogged him throughout his youth. It was not Parmenion who had to be outshone, but Philip whose prestige and success must be surpassed. Nevertheless, although this may have been the psychological moment to reject Darius' offer of peace, Alexander's decision must also have been founded on weighty political, military and economic considerations. Since events are never as enthralling as their background, it may be useful to make a brief examination of Alexander's assorted motives.

We need do little more than glance at the map to see why Alexander found the Euphrates an unsatisfactory frontier. The Persians had pursued an anti-Hellenic policy for a hundred and fifty years, and their defeat was unlikely to bring about a change of heart. The fact that Babylon stood on the east bank of the Euphrates and would have become a frontier city might, at this juncture in history, have served the cause of peace. On the other hand, the territory between there and the Mediterranean coast would have been constantly exposed to attack from High Iran, whereas the core of Persia's dominions was admirably protected from attack by the Zagros Mountains. All in all, the Euphrates would have been an unstable frontier from the military point of view.

Alexander's plan to disseminate Hellenic civilization throughout the world was not primarily directed at the ancient peoples of Mesopotamia. The Persians had been uppermost in his mind from the first. They were a young nation, and nearer the Macedonians in character than any other people in the East. Finally, Egypt, Syria and Mesopotamia were reasonably familiar to the Greeks of Alexander's day. The really alluring prospect was the distant one that lay beyond the Zagros Mountains.

Alexander incorporated the occupied territories in his new order by a series of constitutional enactments, restored the civil service and system of tax-collection, and secured his army's lines of supply. Then, in the summer of 331, he once more took the field against Darius. This campaign was to last until 325 – seven long years of hardship and bloodshed spent among the steppes, snow-clad mountains, jungles and deserts of the world's largest continent.

The Macedonian army marched northwards along the Orontes, then westwards along the foot of the Armenian mountains, crossed the Tigris, and made renewed contact with the enemy outside Gaugamela. The Persians had found no difficulty in raising a second army larger than the one which had been defeated at Issus. The Persian Empire's reserves were, in a very real sense, unlimited. Mobilization of the mounted tribesmen of East Iran, Bactria and Sogdiana had given the Persians a substantial superiority over the Macedonians in the cavalry arm so essential to the conduct of warfare in these wide open spaces. Alexander's army, which was not much larger than it had been at the Granicus, consisted of roughly forty thousand foot-soldiers and seven thousand cavalrymen. It could not be said that the Persians' numerical superiority was overwhelming, since it was they who were overwhelmed. Alexander was now an experienced commander. His soldiers had won two major victories and captured numerous fortified positions, they were veterans, and their morale was unshakeable. Darius laboured under a disadvantage in that Issus was his only practical lesson on how to extract tactical benefits from immense numerical superiority. Numerical superiority does, in fact, breed a false sense of security, and failure breeds panic in such cases. In addition, Darius presented his adversary with the greatest of all tactical advantages – a chance to take the initiative. It was Alexander who attacked. He won his third battle, but it was a near thing. If Alexander had been in Darius' place, Gaugamela would have been a Persian victory. Darius turned tail and fled once more, but this time Alexander had to abandon the chase because the battle was only half won. Only Darius' wing had been routed. Alexander turned about because there was a risk that the other Persian wing, which Parmenion had so far failed to defeat, would rob him of his foregone victory. Darius fled accompanied only by a handful of loyal friends and a small detachment of light cavalry from the steppes. Changing horses repeatedly, he hurried through the Bisutun Pass, the Gateway of Asia, and made for Ecbatana.

Mesopotamia lay at Alexander's feet. Babylon opened its gates to him and he rode into the city amid universal rejoicing. He made sacrifice to the local gods and decreed the rebuilding of the temple of Marduk, which had been destroyed by the Persians.

Having granted his army a brief rest, Alexander moved on to Susa, another Achaemenid seat which yielded vast quantities of plunder; henceforward, Alexander's resources were unlimited. Large quantities of the gold which had been lying fallow in the Persian treasury were minted into coins on his orders. He also abolished the Achaemenid monetary units and introduced the Attic ratio of exchange between gold and silver. Although nothing would have been gained by hoarding the newly minted coins, Alexander began to squander his wealth. Injudicious critics have tried to ascribe his extravagances, which do occasionally seem rather daring, to megalomania. In reality, he acted precisely as if he had studied modern economic theory. The gold put into circulation by his prodigality very soon brought economic life in the recently conquered territories to an unprecedented prosperity.

Alexander had now, by his own efforts, conquered more than Darius had been willing to cede to him. The whole of Mesopotamia belonged to him, but the military situation was still unsatisfactory. It could not have been said, even after the annihilation of the second and larger Persian army, that Darius had run out of alternatives. High Iran was still the core of the Persian Empire, and beyond it loomed the vast and limitless expanse of Asia. Alexander's victory continued to 'smoulder', as Droysen so aptly puts it. After careful consideration, he decided to continue his onslaught on the Achaemenid Empire. Crossing the Zagros Mountains east of Susa by launching a night attack in a blizzard, he occupied Persis, the hub of Achaemenid sovereignty, together with the royal residence of Persepolis and the ancient coronation city of Pasargadae.

Alexander lingered in Persepolis for a long time. He even used it as his base for another thrust eastwards against Carmania, the country to which he was to return after his exertions in India. Meanwhile, Darius remained at Ecbatana. When Alexander finally marched northwards in the hope of forcing a decision under the walls of the city, Darius took flight for the third time. With grim determination, Alexander pursued his luckless adversary eastwards, half-way across the country, but he was not destined to capture him alive. To save their own skin, Darius' companions eventually deserted their lord and master. A Macedonian soldier found the unfortunate man lying abandoned in an ox-cart, mortally wounded by a number of spear-thrusts. All Alexander could do when he arrived shortly afterwards was to cover the dead king with his own cloak. He gave orders that the body should be handed over to the queen mother, Sisygambis, so that she could bury him as befitted his rank. There was no doubt in Alexander's mind that it was his duty to avenge Darius. Regicide had to be punished. His own royal status demanded this, but it was also a political necessity within the context of his plan to assert himself as a legitimate successor of the Achaemenids.

Before going in pursuit of Bessus, the chief regicide, Alexander restored order in Hyrcania, the province bordering the south-east corner of the Caspian Sea. He began by leading an expedition against the tribes inhabiting the southern shores of the Caspian, tribes which the Achaemenids had never subdued even though they had built a royal residence in the area. The natives fled into the virgin forests which clothed the northern slopes of the Elburz Range, where bears and leopards can still be found to this day, and were pursued until they surrendered.

Alexander's time in Hyrcania coincided with an attack on Macedonia by King Agis of Sparta which his loyal viceroy, Antipater, put down. The decisive battle, a confrontation between the traditional fighting spirit of Sparta and the new fighting spirit of Macedonia, was the most sanguinary in Greek history and among those who fell was King Agis himself. But Alexander paid little heed to events in Greece; his empire had attained such proportions that not even a defeat in Hellas would have put his recent conquests in jeopardy. He resumed his advance to the east.

Alexander's original intention had been to march into Bactria by the route which lay north of the Hindu Kush, but this was not to be; a rebellion broke out in the satrapy of Areia, on his right flank, forcing him to return. This insurrection in territory which had already been pacified gave the Macedonians a foretaste of what awaited them in the steppes. The time of dazzling triumphs was past. Force of circumstance, that relentless taskmaster, had long been preparing for this bitter moment. The smouldering discontent of Alexander's generals at his manner of dealing with the Persians found expression in a conspiracy in the course of which Philotas, Parmenion's eldest son, was sentenced to death for high treason by a military tribunal and executed. Alexander at once sent some trustworthy officers to Ecbatana with orders to kill Parmenion on the spot. The old general was stabbed to death while reading a letter from his king. There was a terrible logic in the act. Parmenion's other two sons had lost their lives in Alexander's service, so there was a grave risk that he might turn renegade himself. But, however justified Alexander's concern may have been, the old man's elimination was an act of murder.

The Euphrates in the mountains of Kurdistan

That autumn, Alexander marched via Kandahar to Kabul, swinging southwards in a wide arc. Six thousand feet up in the foothills of the Hindu Kush, the army wintered peacefully in cool fresh mountain air and sparkling sunshine. The year 329 dawned.

The army's withdrawal from Egypt had taken place in the late summer of 331. As at Gordium, two years earlier, Alexander took his time. He curbed his impetuosity and showed himself to be more than just a brilliant general. He took as lively an interest in the welfare of his men as he did in paymasters' strong-boxes and generals' baggage. Once, when short of pack-animals, he burnt an enormous pile of personal effects, his own included. Alexander was prudent and far-sighted, nothing escaped his attention. While in Egypt he introduced some major financial innovations. Hitherto so short of funds that he had been able to make do with a single treasury, he now divided it into a war-chest and a general fund for the civil administration and established central treasuries in Egypt and Syria. His monetary manipulations were so skilful that they later provided the bankers of Alexandria with the basis of a system of international credit which functioned excellently for hundreds of years.

The scope and thoroughness of Alexander's preparations for the next phase of the war suggest that he had a fairly accurate idea of the magnitude and duration of the forthcoming campaign. The time he allowed himself naturally benefited his opponent as well. Darius was able to raise another army at leisure, but Alexander may have regarded this as an advantage. The more completely the enemy managed to mobilize his reserves, the greater the ensuing victory. Of course, Alexander did not yet realize the military significance of wide open spaces. He relied on the tactical virtues of the Macedonian phalanx, on the courage of his battle-hardened veterans, and on the twice-proved superiority of his operational leadership.

Postponement of the army's departure until the summer brought a climatic advantage in its train. The first part of the route led northwards between the Lebanon and Anti-Lebanon ranges, up the valley of the Orontes, which is not unduly hot even in midsummer. The army did not traverse the northern part of the Syrian desert until September, skirting the foot of the Armenian mountains for the sake of water-supplies. Darius made no attempt to obstruct Alexander's crossing of the Euphrates. Indeed, he was so reluctant to fight the next battle with his back to a river and a desert that he assembled his forces beyond the Tigris – a dangerously defeatist course of action coloured by the idea of retreat.

Like the Nile, Ganges and Hoangho, the Euphrates and Tigris are rivers fraught with great historical significance. Mesopotamia, the Land of the Two Rivers, was the birthplace of one of mankind's earliest civilizations. The Euphrates is over 1,700 miles long, rising in Armenia on the western slopes of the massif of which Mount Ararat, Noah's mountain, forms the centre. In Kurdistan the Euphrates is still a narrow, swift-flowing torrent. The middle reaches of the Euphrates and Tigris serve to irrigate the surrounding country and, finally, both rivers combine to form the Shatt el-Arab, a broad and powerful stream which discharges its waters into the Persian Gulf. In the days of the Achaemenids, the Euphrates and Tigris still flowed into the sea through different mouths.

The Persians had constructed barricades not far from the estuaries of the two rivers. Even though the Ionian sea captain Skylax had sailed to the Red Sea from the mouth of the Indus as long ago as the reign of Darius the Great, the Persians were still filled with dread by the immensity of the ocean. Not being a seafaring nation, they feared its unknown expanses as a potential source of attack.

Middle reaches of the Euphrates

Gold chariot from the Oxus Treasure

Alexander crossed the Euphrates at Thapsacus by means of two
swiftly constructed bridges, a fact which conveys some idea of the
scope of the army's engineering equipment. He then learned that
Darius had stationed himself with a huge army on the other side of
the Tigris. Not wishing to make the crossing under enemy fire, he
turned northwards again and crossed the river without loss. What
followed was the battle of Gaugamela, the last of the major battles
between Alexander and the Persians. Its date, 30 September 331, can
be calculated from the lunar eclipse referred to in chroniclers' accounts.
Gaugamela was a cavalry battle whose outcome depended more on
horseflesh than human courage. Techniques of warfare had undergone
a long process of development since the Sumerians invented the
chariot in the first half of the third millennium BC. The Hittites were
great charioteers. The chariot appeared in Egypt and at Mycenae
during the sixteenth century BC and simultaneously in Northern
Europe and China from about 1500 BC onwards. The last people to
use war-chariots, as Caesar mentions in his *Gallic War*, were the Celts.
The gold chariot, a masterpiece from the Oxus Treasure, has large
spoked wheels which were probably capable of crossing quite uneven

Persepolis. Tributary procession

Mounted figure. Achaemenid bronze

Hoplite and cavalryman in combat.
Achaemenid seal impression

190

terrain. The tribesmen of East Iran took to the horse in about 1000 BC, but it was not until the end of the eighth century that the use of horses became widespread. Darius' swarms of mounted tribesmen from the steppes were brilliant horsemen with a long tradition behind them, and superior to Alexander's Thessalian cavalry regiments.

The horses were small but strong and wiry and they must have had extremely tough hoofs, since shoes were still unknown. The Panje horses of Russia are the breed which most closely resembles them today. The frieze from Persepolis also shows how small the horses were, as does the bronze Iranian cavalryman in the British Museum. Riding was a doubly difficult art in those days as the stirrup was not invented until much later, probably by the Parthians. A seal impression of the Achaemenid era clearly illustrates the superiority of the cavalryman over the foot-soldier. It avails the hoplite nothing that he has toted his shield around with him for so many years: the unfortunate man has only a few seconds to live. We know from finds in graves that the Chinese of the T'ang period also used the ponies favoured by Eurasian steppe-warriors, even though they had bred larger strains in the course of the centuries. In terms of artistic merit, the clay horses of the T'ang dynasty are undoubtedly superior to war-horses of every age and breed!

Darius had mustered large bodies of cavalry and drawn up scythed chariots in readiness, and he also had elephants at his disposal. The

China. Clay horse of the T'ang period

tactical effect of elephants on an army unfamiliar with them was not unlike that of tanks in the First World War. They spread terror rather than destruction. Once the driver of one of these mighty beasts had been killed, it was virtually useless. The worst problem – and one which has never been remedied to this day – was that horses detest the smell of elephants.

Tactically, the battle of Gaugamela followed an entirely different pattern from the battle of Issus. No two battles in the history of the world have ever been alike; Napoleon went so far as to say that he had never learnt anything from one battle which he could apply to the next.

Alexander had learnt from Issus. However numerically superior the Persian army might be, however far the Persian battle-line might overlap the Macedonians on each flank, and however great the danger of a Persian cavalry attack from the rear across open terrain, the huge Persian army had an Achilles' heel: the morale of its royal commander-in-chief. Alexander's aim was to hit Darius as hard as he could, and in order to achieve this he employed a tactical ruse.

As at Issus, the king commanded the right wing and Parmenion the left, but instead of attacking leftwards in the direction of Darius and the centre, as might have been expected, Alexander moved by stages to the right. This in itself was enough to confuse the enemy, who realized that it must portend something. Before the significance of the Macedonian manoeuvre became clear, it was too late. The Persians were so preoccupied with the danger of being outflanked that they imitated Alexander's manoeuvre. Their left flank edged progressively to the left until a gap opened in their line. This was just what Alexander had hoped to achieve. He burst through the gap and, at the head of his cavalry, hurled himself at the massed troops who were shielding the Persian king. Darius again threw in his hand prematurely at the crucial moment. What happened then was a repetition of Issus. The Persian right wing had almost won the day against Parmenion. Alexander's tactics produced exactly the same effect on the Macedonian army as they had on the enemy. Parmenion's wing had been unable to maintain contact with Alexander's, and a gap had opened in the Macedonian ranks. The Persian cavalry charged into it, but the Macedonians, whose nerves were stronger, took counter-measures which rendered the enemy's efforts useless.

One small but noteworthy reminder of the battle of Gaugamela is a carved plaque of yellow marble dating from the time of the Emperor Tiberius. Unearthed by Prince Chigi on one of his estates in 1780, it

The Chigi Relief.
Battle of
Gaugamela

is now preserved in the Palazzo Chigi in Rome. The piece, shown here actual size, is only fourteen centimetres deep and nine wide, but its diminutive surface carries a wealth of symbolism. The inscription tells us that the circular medallion, which is raised above an altar in Alexander's honour, represents the cavalry battle at Gaugamela. The two female figures are those of Europe and Asia. Alexander would have been delighted to note that the artist made little distinction between the two continents. Asia wears sandals and an arm-band, whereas Europe is barefoot and unadorned.

Babylon. Reconstruction by Fischer von Erlach

Alexander's fears that the heavily fortified city of Babylon would force him to undertake a long and arduous siege were dispelled by the warmth of his jubilant reception. Mazaeus, the satrap of Babylon, had decided to surrender the city. This was a direct consequence of Darius' flight. Mazaeus had fought bravely at Gaugamela and would have demonstrated his continuing loyalty if Darius had made up his mind to defend Babylon. However, now that Darius had abandoned the rich and fertile land of Mesopotamia without a struggle and withdrawn to the east of his kingdom, the Mesopotamian satraps felt that they had been betrayed by their own king. What made it easier for them to come to terms with their conqueror was that, as past experience showed, Alexander rewarded submission with clemency. Those who resisted him incurred punishment, often of the harshest kind. Alexander confirmed Mazaeus in his appointment and shortly afterwards did the same for Abulitus, the satrap of Susa, who had also surrendered his city and all its riches. These measures prove that Alexander never meant to subject the Achaemenid Empire to alien Macedonian rule. His humane attitude is all the more remarkable in view of the totally different course recommended by his distinguished tutor, Aristotle, who advised him to be 'a leader to the Greeks, a master to the barbarians; to treat the Greeks as friends and kinsmen, the barbarians as if they were beasts or plants . . .'

Aristotle hardly shines in this respect. For once, the soldier was the humanist and the scholar full of arrogance. The obstinacy with which Alexander pursued his plan to merge victors and vanquished and place them on an equal footing was, of course, the source of all the troubles which reached their dramatic climax in the mutiny of his Macedonian veterans after the return from India. For the moment, however, the troops savoured their victory. Fischer von Erlach has left us a vivid artist's impression of Babylon. Although his drawing does not correspond exactly with the results of archaeological research, it is based on accounts given by the ancient writers. The river is the Euphrates; beside the tower in the background stood the temple of Marduk, known to the Romans as Jupiter Baal, the hanging gardens of Semiramis are readily identifiable.

The army needed a breathing-space after the rigours of the march from Egypt to the Tigris and the exertions of the battle of Gaugamela. The soldiers must have been dazzled by their weeks in Babylon. Although covered with scars and glory, the Macedonian veterans hailed from remote mountain valleys in the Balkans and had never before set eyes on an international metropolis. So this was Bab-ilu,

196

the Gate of God, of which so many fabulous tales were told. Babylon was the largest city in the contemporary world, with a population of more than a million. It had eight gates and walls over eleven miles long. Indians, Arabs, Armenians, Phoenicians, Scythians and Ethiopians, all in their different costumes, met and mingled within the confines of the city. In the vaulted bazaars, simple soldiers could feast their eyes on the world's riches: incense, myrrh, gold, ivory, silver-plated harness, jewellery, ointments, purple cloth, and – probably, even at this early date – silk from China. The Babylonians, understandably relieved to be befriended by their mighty conqueror rather than besieged by him, were full of charm and lavish in their hospitality – and, as in every age, Babylon had a host of beautiful and exotically painted women who plied the troops with smiles of welcome. Magnificent buildings; the Gate of Ishtar, faced with glazed tiles on which gorgeous mythical beasts were depicted in a variety of colours; the processional route, bordered by palaces, which led to the ziggurat, the stepped tower at whose summit the deity was worshipped in a small but richly adorned temple; the palace of Nebuchadnezzar (Colour Plate X); the gardens of Semiramis – all these things made an impression, not only on unsophisticated Macedonian peasant-boys and herdsmen's sons, but even on the supercilious Greeks. The riverside road at the foot of the city wall was the place to which the Jews retired during the Babylonian Captivity when the city was celebrating its great religious festivals – the place beside the waters of Babylon where they sat down and wept. They were not lamenting their loss of freedom, since many of them remained in Babylon after Cyrus the Great had given them permission to return home. The object of their lamentation was the ruined Temple of Solomon in Jerusalem. Today, the place of lamentation is the Wailing Wall, which supports the terrace on which the first and second temples of Yahweh both stood in their day. (The Arabs refused to allow any Jew to visit the Wailing Wall between 1948 and 1967.)

Babylon made so profound an impression on Alexander that he decided to make it the capital of his empire. He took his time, however. Most men might have felt inclined to relax after the hardships of the campaign and the fierce excitement of battle, but Alexander at once devoted himself to a pastime which, though truly royal, was scarcely relaxing. He loved lion-hunts, and the Achaemenids had owned vast game reserves in which the beasts were allowed to roam free. During one hunting expedition Alexander was attacked by a lion. Craterus, who was escorting him, fearlessly hurled himself at the dangerous

beast and killed it. The idea of a king being attacked by a lion was well calculated to stir the contemporary imagination. The lion was an animal familiar to the bards of the Homeric age and continued to be a favourite subject among artists until the sixth century BC. Then, with the spread of civilization, it vanished from the Hellenic domain and ceased to figure in any but mythological scenes. From the time of Alexander onwards, the lion-hunt once more became a theme favoured by artists. A late fourth-century relief illustrating the sport was found at Messene in the Peloponnese. A potter's mould unearthed at Arezzo in Tuscany bears a particularly graphic representation of the same theme. The lion has already driven its claws into the shoulder of one of the three huntsmen. The mosaic of the lion-hunt at Pella (Colour Plate II) has been discussed above. Of special note is a carnelian intaglio which Sir Arthur Evans, the excavator of Knossus in Crete, found in a London antique dealer's establishment. This depicts a compact group consisting of two men and a lion. The high standard of composition indicates that the piece is a reproduction of the bronze group which Craterus commissioned from Lysippus and Leochares after Alexander's death and dedicated to the shrine at Delphi. There are many surviving descriptions of this work of art, which was well known in the ancient world. The reproduction is taken from an article published in 1899. The piece itself has since been lost.

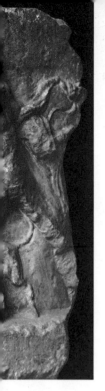

Messene. Relief of
a lion-hunt

Carnelian intaglio of ▶
a lion-hunt

Arezzo. Pottery mould of a lion-hunt

Susa. Tomb of the prophet Daniel

IX   Procession of warriors. Detail from a frieze of glazed tiles in Darius' palace at Susa

Looking down at Susa from an aeroplane is like looking down at six thousand years of history. The debris of nine separate cities, piled one on top of the other, went to make up this gigantic rubbish-dump. The strange building on the large hill in the centre resembles a Crusader castle but is, in fact, an archaeologists' stronghold. The Crusaders never got as far as here, but the men who unearthed the wonders of Susa had to protect themselves against the Bedouins of the surrounding desert. One of the open spaces studded with truncated columns was the paved floor of the palace in which Alexander ceremonially ascended the throne of the Achaemenids. The pointed white cone on the left crowns the mosque erected by the Moslems above the tomb of the prophet Daniel. His fame has withstood the passage of time longest of all. The first reference to his tomb in our own era was made as early as the fourteenth century by the Persian historian Mustaufi.

Susa's origins go back to about 4000 BC. It would be interesting to know how much the new conqueror of the city knew about its history. 'Shush' was founded by the Elamites, a people of unknown stock but one which possessed its own language, script, and art. Elamite art had sunk into oblivion, but the language and script were still in use. In about 1900 BC – as any Jewish scribe could have told Alexander – a ruler from Susa put an end to the Third Dynasty of Ur. It was shortly before this attack on Ur that Abraham left the city of his fathers. Alexander may also have been familiar with the name of King Hammurabi, another monarch who lived in the first half of the second millennium BC. It was the laws of Hammurabi, king of the Amorites, on which Cyrus the Great based the legal code which was still in force in Alexander's day. One thing which Alexander did not know was that the basalt stele on which Hammurabi had his laws inscribed lay buried deep in the ground beneath his throne. Had he realized this, his curiosity would no doubt have prompted him to dig it up and so become the first noted archaeologist in history. The dark basalt stele bears the laws of Hammurabi inscribed in cuneiform, a script whose beauty is well illustrated by the lower of the two photographs on the opposite page. Now in the Louvre, the stele was brought to Susa by King Sutruk Nahhunte I, who acquired it during a raid on Northern Mesopotamia in 1170 BC. It was buried when the Assyrian king Assurbanipal captured Susa in 645 BC and added between three and six feet to the existing mound of debris by razing the city to the ground. A hundred years later the Achaemenids rebuilt Susa and made it their winter residence. The Book of Esther contains a detailed description of one of the great festivals which they celebrated there.

X   *Glazed tiles on an ornamented wall in the throne-room of the Old Palace at Babylon*

Susa. Aerial photograph ▶

Three major roads converged on Susa: the royal highway, with its
one hundred and eleven relay stations, leading to Sardis; a second
road leading north-eastwards to Ecbatana; and a third running eastwards across the Zagros Mountains to Persepolis.

The pottery beaker with the wonderful geometrical design and
stylized animals, probably camels, is a work of art dating from the
year 3500 BC. The large bronze plaque, representing a religious ceremony, dates from the twelfth century BC and originated in the reign
of King Shilhak-Inshushinak.

Susa. Stele bearing the laws of Hammurabi, with a detail from its cuneiform inscription, c. 1900 BC

Susa. Bull capital, c. 500 BC.

Susa. Winged lion in glazed tiles, c. 500 BC

The bull capital, the magnificent winged lion and the relief of a procession of warriors in glazed tiles (Colour Plate IX) are Achaemenid. The warriors, with their sternly martial bearing and measured tread, still adorned the palace walls in Alexander's day. Among other items found at Susa by Alexander were the bronze effigies of Harmodius and Aristogeiton dating from the end of the sixth century. These two friends had assassinated the tyrant Hipparchus, who ruled Athens jointly with his brother Hippias, and the Athenians had erected a monument in their honour. Xerxes carried off both statues when he plundered Athens, not for the sake of their renowned beauty but as a kind of symbolic hold over the Athenians. Alexander returned the treasured works of art to their city of origin. Not many years ago, archaeologists digging in the Athenian agora found a fragment belonging to the inscribed plinth which once supported the statues. The originals have disappeared, and only Roman copies in marble still survive.

Looking through the lofty windows of the throne-room at Susa, Alexander could see the foothills of the Zagros looming on the horizon. These impassable mountains formed a massive rampart which protected High Iran, the heart of the Achaemenid Empire, from its enemies. Beyond them lay the future. Alexander was fully aware that any extension of his sovereignty would necessarily multiply the problems posed by the territories he had already conquered. What increased his difficulties still further was that he always had an eye to the preservation of future peace. To prevent the people of Asia from regarding him as an alien conqueror, the Macedonian king had, if possible, to become the legitimate successor of the Achaemenids. This policy provoked dissension in another quarter. The more Alexander departed from his original status as warrior prince of the Macedonian people, the greater became the opposition of his generals, especially the older ones among them, who belonged to his father's generation.

Alexander's parting gesture before he left Susa was as shrewd as it was magnanimous. Queen Stateira, Darius' wife, had died of grief only a year after Issus. Darius' children and Sisygambis, the queen mother, were permitted to maintain a royal household and granted Susa as their official residence. Their conqueror expressed only one wish: he left some scholars behind with a request that the Persian princesses should learn Greek.

Base of the monument to Harmodius and Aristogeiton, found in the Agora at Athens.
On the right, Roman copies of the statues

The year 331 drew to a close, and 330, the fifth year of war, dawned
over the Zagros. Darius had made no diplomatic overtures since his
defeat at Gaugamela. Persian troops under Ariobarzanes had impreg-
nably fortified the only pass in the south of the Zagros, but Alexander
forced it by means of an outflanking movement. Carried out under
the most arduous and wintry conditions, it was a military operation
which would have taxed modern alpine troops. Persepolis and
Pasargadae, the ancient royal cities, fell into Alexander's hands
together with a third vast haul of gold, silver, and other treasures.
It is said that twenty thousand mules and three thousand camels were
needed to carry these spoils when they were transferred to Ecbatana
at a later stage.

Persepolis. Darius the Great receiving a dignitary

Alexander lingered in Persia for four long months. He may have been expecting another peace offer from Darius now that he had conquered the southern part of High Iran, but nothing happened. Darius went irrevocably to meet his doom.

The superb sculptures at Persepolis provided Alexander with an impressive textbook on the court ceremonial of the empire he planned to make his own. One of them shows a satrap being received in audience by Darius the Great. A blown kiss was the most refined form of homage which the mighty King of Kings could receive from his senior dignitaries. However, Alexander's attempt to introduce Persian ceremonial led to renewed conflicts with the Macedonian and Greek noblemen of his entourage.

Persepolis was the scene of the New Year festival – the greatest religious festival of the year – and the place to which tribute flowed annually from all over the Persian Empire. The peoples of Asia revered it as the sacred seat of Persian power, and the ramifications of that power extended far to the east, as Asoka's column at Sarnath in India still testifies.

It was in the 'Park of the Gazelles' at Sarnath, near Benares, that Buddha preached his first sermon – an event which was already two centuries old in Alexander's day. When the Chinese pilgrim Hsuen Tsang visited Sarnath and its many shrines in AD 640, or almost a thousand years after Alexander's death, it was still at the height of its glory and its monasteries housed fifteen hundred monks. One of the most important relics described by Hsuen Tsang was a column erected by King Asoka, the oriental ruler who did most for Buddhism. Asoka was to Buddhism what Constantine the Great was to Christianity. Sixty years after Alexander's death, he founded an empire which extended from Afghanistan to the Ganges. Comparing Asoka's column with the column beside the Gate of Xerxes or the three bronze lions,

The Asoka column from Sarnath

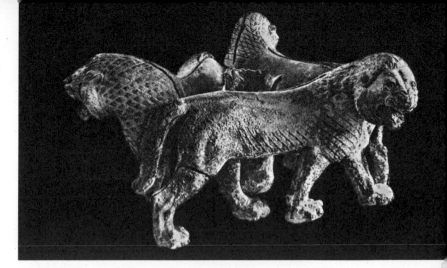

Persepolis. Bronze stand composed of three lions

which also come from Persepolis, one can see that the Indian sculptor was influenced by Achaemenid art. Nothing in the whole of Western art displays such strong traces of Achaemenid influence.

Whatever else one may think of it, the burning of Persepolis on Alexander's orders was a sign to the peoples of Asia. The gods had given their verdict and a new ruler had arisen. The flames that devoured Persepolis destroyed the sanctum of a dynasty which had reigned in splendour for two centuries. That Alexander intended this flaming torch to be a symbol to Asia can be inferred from his order to extinguish the fire as soon as one of the great halls had been burnt down. Traces of burning can still be seen on the bases of the columns.

Persepolis. Base of a column beside the Gate of Xerxes

The army now set out on a series of interminable marches. The countryside through which it passed on its way northwards possesses a grandiose beauty – one might almost call it heroic, though scenery is of secondary importance to heroes on the march. The infantry found it hot and dusty. As for the cavalry, they were far less interested in the

214

sublime spectacle of the sun rising above the distant mountains than in finding water for their horses. The boy driving his two donkeys through the lonely waste may be as free as the wind and frightened of nothing, but he can only eat his fill on major holidays – not more than twice a year. It is a poor land.

Camel train in Iran

XI   *Glass vase from Begram, Afghanistan, representing the Pharos at Alexandria*

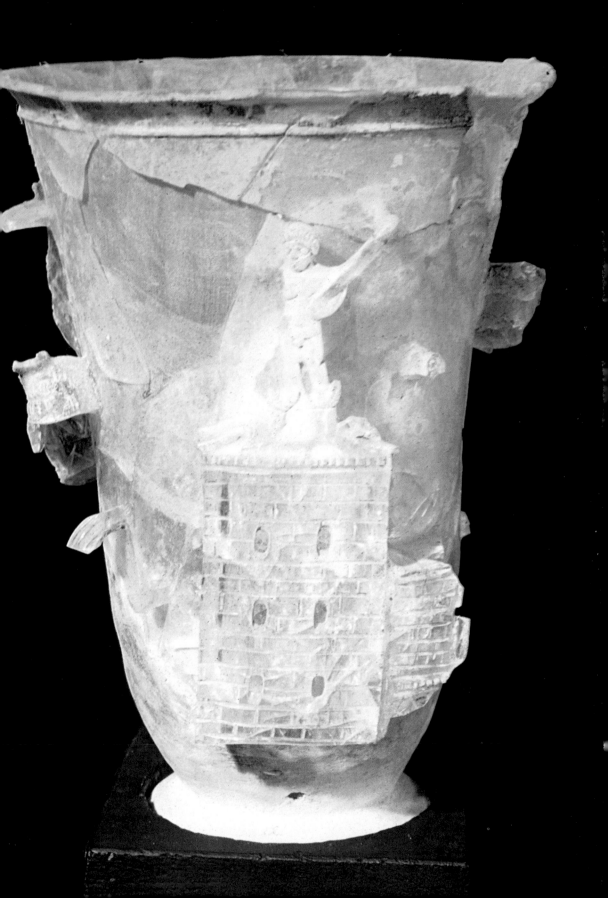

Here and there the Macedonians came across camel trains, until very recent times the sole means of transport in the East. However long they have spent in Asia, people never cease to marvel at these strange, haughty, ill-natured beasts. One of the world's most unforgettable sounds is that made by the bells of the lead-camel as a caravan nears a caravanserai and the starry sky above the steppe turns pale with the approach of dawn. Alexander's troops may also have encountered the odd nomadic tribe trekking across the barren waste with camels, horses and donkeys, their poultry suspended in baskets beneath the camels' bellies, their herds of goats, sheep and cattle trailing a long plume of dust. The black tents of the nomads look vaguely sinister in the immensity of the desert, but the people are extremely hospitable, and it is no hardship to sit on a pile of magnificent rugs inside a chieftain's tent. All this is very much as it was two or three thousand years ago.

Nomads' black tents in the mountains　　　　　*Iran. Nomadic tribe on the move* ▶

217

XII   Devata from Turfan. A sculpture of the Buddhist 'Late Classical' period in Asia, an offshoot of Greek art which lasted until well into the eighth century AD

Alexander's next objective was Ecbatana, now Hamadan, in North-West Iran, where Darius had made a last attempt to raise an army. He was still accompanied by a large number of Persian noblemen. However, apart from a few loyalists who championed the traditional Persian cause, they consisted of the satraps of the eastern territories, who supported Darius in the hope of saving their personal domains from the dreaded invader. This was the only reason why they stood by their hereditary monarch.

Ecbatana was situated on the main caravan route which emerged from Central Asia via Bactria and led, via Babylon, to the Mediterranean. Ancient writers described it as a city of unsurpassed splendour, of temples with silvered roofs, of sumptuous palaces whose halls were adorned with gilded cedar wood, of massive walls surrounded by wonderful gardens. Still referred to in the twelfth century AD as an immense ruined site, Ecbatana and all its splendours have since sunk below ground-level.

221

Hamadan (Ecbatana). Aerial photograph ▶

Achaemenid gold vessel, probably from Hamadan

A new town has grown up on the site. Trudging up and down the narrow lanes of Hamadan, the visitor can still come across hovels in which the kitchen bench consists of a marble step once trodden by the ruler of the world as he entered his palace. One has literally only to turn over the soil with a spade and the most marvellous works of art come to light.

The gold vessel from Ecbatana dates from the sixth century, a period when Achaemenid art was at its zenith. Its twin-headed ibex handles, band of winged lions and rich ornamentation make this piece one of the most highly prized examples of Achaemenid goldsmith's work. The gold platter decorated with a stylized eagle dates from Alexander's time and is also classic in its beauty. Excavations at Ecbatana will sooner or later bring to light something of major significance.

Achaemenid gold platter with stylized eagle

The lion of Hamadan

Hamadan has two reminders of Alexander the Great. The first, a sculptured lion dating from the fourth century BC, probably formed part of a tomb erected in honour of Macedonian soldiers killed in action. The lion's limbless torso lay sprawled on the ground when Flandin and Coste toured Persia in 1851 and seen among the little tufts of grass in the Frenchman's sketch, it looks amiable and not particularly leonine. Luschey established that the Hamadan lion is a companion-piece of the lion of Chaeronea. Re-erected, though not at a sufficiently commanding height, it is now used as a make-believe horse by adventurous local youngsters. The women of Hamadan regard it as a fertility symbol. When they want children, they go 'out to the lion' at twilight and offer it a little honey.

The second reminder, the monument overleaf, silhouetted against the Zagros Mountains, was designed by a modern architect but based on

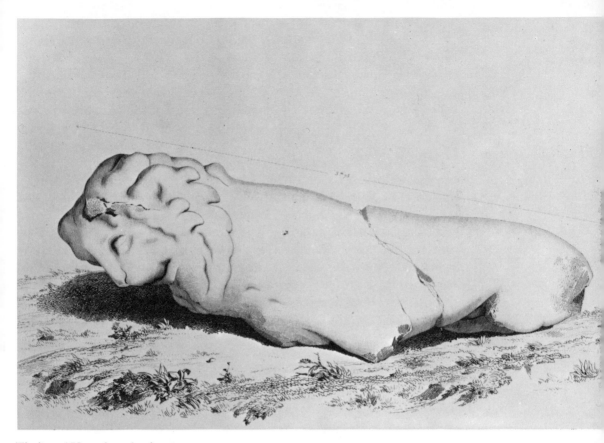

The lion of Hamadan, sketch, 1851

Islamic buildings of the Middle Ages. It stands over the mausoleum of Abu 'Ali al Husain ibn 'Abdallah ibn Sina, known in Europe as Avicenna, who died at Hamadan in AD 1037. Avicenna, an authority on Aristotle, Alexander's tutor, appears in the *Divine Comedy*, where Dante allots him a place not far from Aristotle and between Hippocrates and Galenus, the two most celebrated physicians of the ancient world. It was to his writings that Europe owed the preservation of important items of ancient scientific knowledge, particularly in the field of medicine.

A few days' march from Ecbatana, news came that Darius had abandoned the city and withdrawn his forces to the east. Alexander's disappointment must have been intense. The supposed end of all his labours had proved to be a mirage which vanished into thin air at his approach.

The obvious course was all-out and immediate pursuit of the retreating enemy, but Alexander shunned the obvious. So far, the war had been fought in civilized and familiar countries. What lay ahead was uncharted territory. Alexander had acquired a new and unknown enemy – the endless expanses of Asia. Being a stickler for security, he established a new base at the easternmost extremity of his advance to date. From now on his base of operations was situated, not in Macedonia nor on the Mediterranean coast, but far to the east in Iran itself. Having placed Parmenion in command of the new communications centre, Alexander set off once more. A march of eleven days brought him to Rhagae, a town slightly to the south of Teheran, which was still a village in those days. Towering above the Macedonian army and covered with snow, even in July, stood the Demavend, at almost nineteen thousand feet the highest peak in the Elburz Mountains, which form a barrier between the Caspian and High Iran. After a few days' rest the chase was resumed. Darius had already passed through the Caspian Gates and was on his way to Bactria.

Elburz Mountains.
The Demavend
(18,500 ft)

Hamadan.
Mausoleum of Avicenna

The Caspian Gates

The Macedonians may not have found the terrain entirely unfamiliar, since its alternation of tall barren mountains and small fertile valleys was reminiscent of their homeland. Under such a sun, water is synonymous with paradise. Travelling conditions must have been arduous in the extreme. There is a great difference between getting a herdsman and a handful of cattle across a narrow bridge and using the same bridge to carry forty thousand infantry and six thousand cavalry. With a last titanic effort, Alexander overhauled Darius, but the Persian king's companions had long since put him in chains at the instigation of Bessus, satrap of Bactria. When their pursuers caught up, they had speared their lord and master to death.

Crossing a river in the mountains

Mountain valley—a garden in the wilderness ▶

Steppe east of the Caspian Sea

The next satrapy to be occupied by Alexander was that of Hyrcania on the Caspian Sea. The southern shores of the Caspian also possess great scenic beauty, and the western part – referred to by modern Persians as their Riviera – is subtropical in character. The fishing-boat in the photograph on the left is used for catching sturgeon. (Ancient writers do not tell us whether Alexander and his luxury-loving, gourmandizing noblemen ever sampled caviar.)

Having consolidated his position in Hyrcania, Alexander set off to capture Bessus, the murderer of Darius. After a wearisome march across the steppe which extends from the Caspian to the western foothills of the Hindu Kush, he entered the valley of the Heri Rud. Our aerial photograph conveys some idea of the immensity of the steppe and its infinite melancholy. Alexander called a halt and founded

Caspian Sea with the Elburz Mountains in the background

Alexandria Areion, a place destined to future greatness. Known today as Herat, it rose under the Timurid emperors of the early Middle Ages to become one of the wealthiest cities in Asia. Herat's mosques are famed for their beauty throughout the Islamic world, and its citizens still recall with pride that their city was originally founded by Alexander the Great.

Following the valley of the Helmund on its march to Kabul, the army

Kandahar (Alexandria Arachoton).
The Asoka inscription was found near here

Herat (Alexandria Areion).
In the background, the Hindu Kush

reached Kandahar, which is probably identical with Alexandria Arachoton, another of Alexander's foundations. An inscription discovered near there (p. 177) gives the text of a decree issued by King Asoka in the middle of the third century BC. Written in both Greek and Aramaic, it is the easternmost Greek inscription ever to be found and proves that Greeks were still playing an important role in Afghanistan seventy years after Alexander's death.

At Seistan, in the middle of the Zarin Desert, Italian archaeologists have recently unearthed a town which flourished in the Achaemenid era. The surrounding countryside did not look quite as bleak in those days. One of the problems of modern Persia is that the land is subject to a continuous drying-out process whose origins lie far in the geological past. The deserts of central Iran are slowly but steadily expanding.

The army moved into its winter quarters at Kabul on the south side of the Hindu Kush. Kabul Museum is a historical treasure-house containing a host of precious relics of the country's Greek past, which spanned several centuries. 'Late Classical' Buddhist art of the eighth century AD (see Colour Plate XII) still betrays the influence of Greek artists.

Zarin. Ruins of the ancient capital of the satrapy of Drangiana, dating from Achaemenid times

Begram. Bust of Alexander the Great

The glass vessel originally from Syria, illustrated overleaf, is one of many rare pieces found at Begram, some miles north of Kabul. Also found there was the sculpture illustrated above. Whether or not the handsome youth represents Alexander the Great, this is how the peoples of Asia have continued to think of him down the centuries.

*Begram. Painted glass
vase from Syria*

Early Hellenistic silver disk. War-elephant carrying Macedonian soldiers ►

V *Triumph and Farewell*

THE WINTER OF 330–329, spent at Kabul in the Hindu Kush, was the turning-point in Alexander's life. It was not that the tide of success receded – still less that failure set in. Alexander never experienced such a reversal of fortune. It was the glamour of his regal existence that began to fade. Each success posed new problems. Each exertion on the army's part proved to be no more than a prelude to further hardships. The greater Alexander's power became, the greater became the difficulties of wielding it. The more he endeared himself to the Persians, the more he alienated his former comrades-in-arms. It would not be surprizing if his thoughts turned occasionally to the epic battle between his ancestor Heracles and the Lernean Hydra, a monster which sprouted two serpents' heads in place of every one the hero lopped off. Alexander's strength did not wane. He just became harder, grimmer, and more ferocious in the conduct of war.

It all began with the death of Darius, which did nothing to ameliorate Alexander's position. As long as Darius was alive, he had an enemy he could negotiate with. The two men had known one another as intimately as only enemies of long standing can. For five years, each had tried to read the other's thoughts, wrestled with him in spirit, dreamed of sitting at the same table and drinking the same wine. Now, in place of a man whose royal birth he had respected, Alexander was confronted by a pack of power-hungry and treacherous regicides led by Bessus, satrap of Bactria and a prince of the blood royal. To call them a 'pack' is no exaggeration. They were steppe-wolves who controlled a vast, untamed area threaded with huge mountain chains and bordered by limitless tracts of unknown territory. This was the region that had to be conquered, but the fighting developed into a guerilla war in which it was easier to catch dysentery than earn a modicum of glory.

No place could have been better suited than Kabul to give the conqueror an insight into the geography of Asia. When Alexander emerged from his tent in the morning – an extremely comfortable, extremely regal tent with walls made of fine leather – he found himself facing the Hindu Kush, whose gleaming snow-capped peaks rose to a height of twenty-four thousand feet, forming a massive mountain rampart which shielded North-East Iran from the steppes of Asia. Alexander knew more about what lay beyond that rampart than he had known at Susa about what lay beyond the Zagros. Seven passes led across the Hindu Kush from Kabul to the lands watered by the Oxus, but the lowest of them was six thousand feet up. As for the Khawak Pass, which Alexander eventually used when crossing the range in the spring of 329, this attained a height of eleven thousand six hundred feet. Kabul was 1,750 miles from Ecbatana, or 101 days' march. From Ecbatana to Sardis was another 1,375 miles, and from Sardis to Pella another 560 miles. This meant that Kabul was about 3,700 miles or nine months' march from the Macedonian capital. The only people who could cover such distances in a reasonably short time were couriers entitled to use the royal staging-posts, where relays of fresh horses were always held in readiness.

Having gone thus far, Alexander was destined to go even farther. A march of 750 miles separated Kabul from Khodjend, the northernmost point reached by Alexander during his campaign in the steppes of Central Asia. Here he had founded Alexandria Eschate, or 'farthest' Alexandria. It was almost 500 miles from Kabul to the Hyphasis, the river which marked the limit of his advance into India. The very magnitude of these distances shattered Aegean-style notions of geography. However, Asia had still further surprises in store for Alexander's inquiring mind. He must have realized by the time he reached Kabul, if not before, that the ideas which he had entertained about the dimensions of the earth when he set out from Macedonia – so long ago now – bore no relation to reality. He had to abandon all hope of extending his dominions so far in every direction that no enemy could exist beyond his borders. The northern marches of Persia abutted on countries of unknown size inhabited by autonomous races of unknown strength. The more Alexander learned about India, the more the 'Ocean' receded.

Winter was not over before the first envoys sent by Indian princes arrived at Alexander's court in Kabul. Although the Indus Valley had been subjugated by Darius the Great, the rajahs had regained a large measure of independence over the years. Some of them now solicited Alexander's aid against their enemies. Nothing could have suited him better. If he exploited the rajahs' feuds in the right way, it should not be difficult to gain control of the Punjab. The temptation to make a move – which was all he needed to do – must have been strong indeed. However, although the mighty Hindu Kush shielded High Iran in the north-east, it was no protection to Persia. Between the eastern spurs of the Elburz Mountains and the western spurs of the Hindu Kush lay a gap which would have allowed Bessus to disrupt Alexander's lines of communication at any time he chose. Bessus had meanwhile donned the tiara and assumed the royal name Artaxerxes. What made him such a dangerous enemy was that, as an Achaemenid, he had a legitimate claim to the throne. Alexander had been obliged to defeat Darius, the king. Bessus, the regicide, had to be exterminated.

Alexander reluctantly shelved his dreams of India and, bowing to force of circumstance, turned northwards. In the spring of 329 his army crossed the Hindu Kush. Two years were to pass before he saw Kabul again, and he was not able to set out for India until the spring of 327.

The Furies overtook Bessus with a speed which exceeded Alexander's expectations. As soon as his princely confederates saw that he was just as ineffectual an opponent of Alexander as Darius had been, they abandoned him. Bessus fell into Alexander's hands, was exhibited to the Macedonian army standing naked by the roadside with chains round his neck, then led away and executed.

Spitamenes, a member of the old Bactrian aristocracy, assumed command of the struggle for independence in Transoxiana. He was the ablest opponent Alexander ever encountered. Despite his limited resources, Spitamenes compelled his mighty adversary to wage war for a whole year. He might have continued to fight on undefeated if his unruly allies had not murdered him and sent his severed head to Alexander in the hope of reward.

Alexander, who cherished a lifelong respect for courage, bestowed a posthumous honour on his enemy. At Susa, he arranged a marriage between Seleucus, one of his generals, and Spitamenes' daughter Apame. Seleucus was the only senior officer not to repudiate his Persian wife after Alexander's death. As consort of Seleucus I Nicator, Apame became co-founder of a powerful dynasty which was to defend Alexander's heritage against the Romans a century and a half later.

The army sustained many reverses in the fierce fighting with Spitamenes' partisans during the summer of 329, and tension mounted at

Alexander's headquarters week by week. Philotas' treachery had merely set a precedent. The gradual introduction of Persian court ceremonial had caused bitter resentment among the older Macedonian generals. From Alexander's point of view, this was unavoidable. If he wanted to win over the peoples of the East, he must surround himself with the same pomp and splendour as the Great Kings who had preceded him. Although most of the Macedonian grandees had readily adopted the extravagant ways of Persian satraps, they showed no understanding of Alexander's policy. Cleitus, one of Philip II's former comrades-in-arms, got drunk at a feast in Marakanda and began to abuse Alexander in the most violent terms. Plutarch's description of the scene is based on an eye-witness account, probably given by Ptolemaeus, later King Ptolemy I of Egypt. It is remarkable how much freedom of speech Alexander permitted in his presence. Cleitus had already been hustled outside by friends when he burst in again and launched into an even wilder tirade. The king, who had restrained himself admirably until then, seized a spear and hurled it at Cleitus in a sudden access of fury. His aim was all too accurate. Cleitus gave a fearful cry and fell dead. His sister Lanice had been Alexander's nurse, and he himself had saved Alexander's life at the Granicus. The king was plunged in grief, but the deed was done.

Not long afterwards there was another treason trial. The royal pages hatched a conspiracy in which Aristotle's nephew Callisthenes became so unwisely embroiled that he was condemned to death. It is probable that he died before sentence could be carried out, but Alexander's relationship with his old tutor lost some of its former cordiality and became noticeably cooler.

Many have argued that these two years of fierce and costly warfare, waged against courageous steppe tribesmen who were fighting for their independence, were an immense waste of time and effort. Our attitude is naturally coloured by the realization of how little time remained to Alexander. On the other hand, both Cyrus the Great and, after him, Darius the Great had considered it necessary to construct a defensive rampart against the steppe. Alexander took over the old Persian frontier defences and supplemented them with an extensive network of military posts. These not only served to police the area but acted as centres of defence against external attack. However, Alexander was too shrewd to rely on force of arms alone. He contented himself with defeating the princes and, having defeated them, won them over by his generosity and turned them into allies. The great conqueror ultimately became 'one of them' by marrying Roxana, a Bactrian princess. Roxana was the daughter of Oxyartes, the king whose stronghold in the Karakorum had been one of the last pockets of resistance to be captured by Alexander. The fighting in Bactria had secured Alexander's rear in the fullest possible fashion and paved the way for his Indian campaign, but it had done far more than provide a temporary safeguard for further military operations. His advance to the Jaxartes intimidated the nomadic tribes of Asia so thoroughly that they left Bactria in peace for centuries to come. Alexander's battle with the Scythians shows that he was alive to the psychological efficacy of shock tactics. He had fully decided to make the Jaxartes his frontier and allow the Scythians to retain their freedom, but when they gathered on the opposite bank and began to taunt the Macedonians he crossed the river and engaged them. Much to the amazement of the brilliant Scythian horsemen, who habitually avoided pitched battles by retiring at speed, they were encircled and decisively defeated. The nomadic warriors lost none of their lust for conquest as a result of this defeat and the consequent impossibility of further raids on Bactria. Resorting to another of their usual tactics, they turned their attention to areas where the pickings were easier and began to harass the south. A century after Alexander's death the Chinese emperors found themselves compelled to adopt his methods and fortify their own frontiers against nomadic invasions by building the Great Wall. Another result of lasting peace with the steppe was the blossoming of Greek kingdoms in this part of the world. They endured for many centuries, and recent excavation has revealed the full extent of their influence on the Oriental world of ideas. Their effect on the art of Central Asia could still be felt in the eighth century AD. It found final expression in the monasteries of the Tarim Basin, in a Buddhist 'Late Classical' period which bore a startling resemblance to its Christian counterpart in Western Europe.

Alexander brought his campaign to a triumphant conclusion by conquering the Punjab and leading the 'Voyage of a Thousand Ships' down the Indus from the place where the mighty river emerged from the Himalayas to its estuary in the Indian Ocean. He fought one more successful battle in India – the last major battle of his career – but befriended his wounded and defeated opponent, King Porus, on the battlefield itself. He not only allowed Porus to keep all his territorial possessions but added to them. He did not, however, deprive him of all his enemies. As in Bactria and Transoxiana, Alexander carefully preserved a 'balance of rivalry'. Despite the heavy cost of conquering these territories, he linked them to his empire only by imposing a

loose form of suzerainty on their native rulers. One important conclusion can be drawn from Alexander's restraint. Whatever vague
intention of conquering the world he may have entertained at the
beginning of his career – and there is no evidence that he ever thought
in those terms – he must have abandoned it by the time he reached
India. Alexander never at any stage in his military career embarked
on a new phase of operations without fortifying and securing the
territory already conquered. Under the political constitution granted
it by Alexander, the Punjab could never have formed the basis for
further conquests in India. It is doubtful, therefore, if the withdrawal
from the Hyphasis was forced on him by the mutiny of his army.
Tarn believes that the king positively welcomed the mutiny, and
Koepp, a shrewd nineteenth-century authority on Alexander, goes so
far as to suggest that the whole dramatic conflict took place in the mind
of the king and the imagination of historians.

The event which concluded the Indian campaign was magnificently
real. About a hundred of the ships which Alexander ordered to be
built on the upper reaches of the Indus were seagoing vessels. This
small fleet was to set sail from the mouth of the Indus under the
command of Nearchus, a Cretan, and attempt to reach the Persian
Gulf by following the southern shores of Iran. This opened up the
sea-route between the Middle and Far East. Within an astonishingly
short space of time, trade began to flourish on a truly worldwide scale,
linking the Mediterranean with India by sea and India by caravan with
Afghanistan, Bactria, the Tarim Basin, and China. Although Nearchus
himself lost few ships during his voyage across the uncharted Ocean,
the cost of this venture was extremely high.

The bulk of the army, together with the wounded, the elephants and
supply train, had been entrusted to Craterus and sent back across the
Mulla Pass, which lay a little farther to the north. Marching by way
of Kandahar in Arachosia and through Seistan, Craterus safely reached
the peaceful and fertile land of Carmania, east of Persepolis. Alexander
himself marched along the coast through Gedrosia in order to support
Nearchus' seaborne expedition by digging wells and establishing supply depots. It was late in August 325 when he set off. Alexander's last
trek through Gedrosia to Carmania was the most arduous of his
entire ten-year campaign. Having advanced along the coast for only
a short distance, the army was compelled to strike north by the nature
of the terrain. During the sixty-day march through the desert, hunger,
thirst and heat robbed Alexander of three-quarters of his men – at a
conservative estimate, somewhere between twenty and thirty thousand

of his best troops. When it finally reached its destination, the army that had conquered the world was reduced to a rabble of ragged, emaciated, bare-footed, virtually unarmed men, covered with sores and accompanied by a few wretched-looking horses. Alexander shared his soldiers' hardships to the last. One wonders what he must have thought of military glory as he watched the relics of his all-conquering army totter past.

Alexander had accomplished the grand design with which he left the royal palace at Pella in 334. He had conquered the Achaemenid Empire, secured his frontiers and brought his army back, but the time for celebration had not yet arrived.

Ever insistent on security, Alexander always did his best to pacify conquered territory before embarking on new operations. Wherever Persians had remained in senior posts or been entrusted with satrapies by him, he curbed their power by making them work in harness with Macedonian military commanders. These far-sighted measures ensured that, for all the unrest which was necessarily occasioned in vast and newly conquered territories by a radical transformation of the political and economic *status quo*, no really serious threat to Macedonian sovereignty ever presented itself. Even so, disorder had gradually assumed sizeable proportions. Extravagance, corruption, oppression, and the recruitment of small armies of mercenaries by local military commanders – all these abuses had begun to spread in a deplorable way, nor was lack of discipline confined to Persians in senior positions. Alexander's own treasurer, Harpalus, a scion of the princely house of Elimiotes and one of the king's boyhood friends, had fled with an enormous sum of money after scandalous goings-on with the loveliest and most expensive courtesans in Athens. Although naturally inclined to generosity and forgiveness, Alexander found himself compelled to mete out severe penalties. Many death sentences were imposed. At last, before the king left Carmania and set out for Susa, victory celebrations were held. From that moment onwards, the tempo of Alexander's life began to accelerate in a singular manner.

Whatever one's verdict on Alexander, there is no doubt that he possessed imagination. The conquest of the East was complete. Whether it was final and whether he would be forced to take up arms again were questions which even he may have been unable to answer. At all events, he now became preoccupied with the vision of a merger between the civilizations of the West and East, the process which historians later christened Hellenism. The means which Alexander employed in the furtherance of his plans ranged from the beauty of

Iranian women to the training methods of the Macedonian phalanx. He himself married an Achaemenid princess, Darius' eldest daughter Stateira, and turned the wedding into a ceremony which must be unique in the history of the world. He married off most of his senior officers to attractive Persian girls of noble birth and granted ten thousand of his soldiers permission – and a financial inducement – to wed Persian women. At the same time, he gave orders that thirty thousand Persian youths who had undergone instruction in Macedonian tactics should be enrolled in the army on the same footing as Macedonians.

The mass wedding at Susa created ten thousand miniature theatres of war which served the cause of peace. The enrolment of the young Persians resulted in a mutiny by the entire army, but Alexander did not lose his grip. Having seen for himself that the army was the best possible 'school for Hellenism', he destroyed his father's creation – the army with which he had conquered Asia – at the very moment when its narrow nationalistic attitude began to interfere with his plans. His political foresight was as remarkable in this respect as his complete lack of old soldier's sentimentality.

The court moved to Ecbatana. No one could have begrudged Alexander the opportunity to relax and enjoy the fruits of his labours, if only for a short while, but fate chose this moment to deal him a frightful blow. Hephaestion fell ill and died within the space of a few days – Hephaestion, the only real friend Alexander had ever possessed and probably the only man who grasped Alexander's true greatness during his lifetime. Genius is a solitary quality, and its solitude is shrouded in silence. The king was inconsolable. Just as he had always regarded Hephaestion as his Patroclus, so his mind became darkened by a premonition that Achilles' hour would also strike before long.

His premonition was well founded.

From Babylon, Alexander organized a large-scale expedition which was to explore and open up the sea-route from the Persian Gulf to the Red Sea. While engaged in these preparations, he succumbed to a fever of only a few days' duration – probably malaria.

A few grains of quinine would have saved the king's life, but the quinquina tree was unknown in Alexander's empire. His body was embalmed, laid out on a sumptuously decorated hearse, and transported with great pomp and splendour to Egypt. The funeral procession took weeks to reach its destination. Alexander was later buried in a glass sarcophagus at Alexandria, where his mortal remains continued to be venerated for centuries.

The Khawak Pass in spring-time ▶

*Ravine giving access
to one of the passes
in the Hindu Kush*

Alexander began his arduous and hard-fought campaign in the broad
steppes of Asia with a military feat of great daring. A hundred years
before Hannibal crossed the Alps, he negotiated the Hindu Kush by
way of a pass which was considerably higher than the one which took
the Carthaginian army into Italy. He chose the Khawak, the most
easterly of the seven passes which led from Kabul to the lowlands of
the Oxus. At this point, only a few hundred miles separated the army
from the Sinkiang border. Tactical considerations dictated the choice
of the Khawak, which was also the highest and most extensively
snowbound of the seven passes. Bessus, who was using modern
'scorched earth' tactics, had transformed the rich and fertile country

between the northern slopes of the Hindu Kush and the Oxus into a desert. However, his depredations did not extend far enough eastwards to jeopardize the Macedonian army's supplies. Bessus had discounted the possibility that Alexander might select the most difficult pass of all. When he learned that his awe-inspiring and apparently irresistible foe had reached Drapsaka, east of Bactra, with his army intact, he was seized with panic. Abandoning his well-laid plans for the defence of Bactria, he fled across the Oxus into Transoxiana.

The photograph on the left shows how difficult it is to negotiate these rugged mountains. Even today, melting snow and rainstorms flood the narrow road, which is little better than the caravan track of long ago, and the way is often barred by rock-falls. It is not hard to imagine how practical it would have been to defend such a narrow ravine. The photograph of Band-i-Amir, a lake situated high in the mountains, shows us a primeval landscape. The lake itself is a glowing emerald-green. The pass, a narrow track leading through the wilderness, was deep in snow when the Macedonian army crossed it.

A pleasant anecdote is told of this march through the mountains, which lasted a fortnight. At the end of one exhausting day, Alexander

The Band-i-Amir, a lake situated more than 6,000 feet up in the Hindu Kush

was sitting beside a camp fire on a small chair which had been transported across the mountains on donkey-back. His men were hungry, dazzled by the glare of sun on snow-fields by day, and chilled to the marrow by night. While he was sitting warming his hands he saw a veteran who had been with him at the Granicus totter towards the fire, half snow-blind. The king rose and urged the old man to sit down on his chair. Having thawed out, the soldier suddenly recognized Alexander, who was squatting beside him in the snow. He jumped up with a start, but Alexander merely smiled and said: 'If you had sat on the King of Persia's chair it would have meant death. Because it is Alexander's chair, you are restored to life.' Stories of this kind spread quickly through the ranks, re-establishing Alexander's original status as warrior prince of Macedonia. He may have regained some of his youthful *joie de vivre* as a result, but his men were less happy. Quite apart from their renewed privations and hardships, they resented the fact that Alexander was incorporating more and more Asiatics in his forces. Co-operation between Macedonians and native troops under battle conditions was just what Alexander was relying on to bring about a gradual fusion, but his hopes were not realized until a generation later.

The Bactrian cavalry, brilliant horsemen who had fought bravely at Gaugamela, defected from Bessus when he took flight. Some of them dispersed, but many went over to Alexander and were promptly enrolled in his army. Alexander occupied the whole area between the Hindu Kush and the Oxus without undue difficulty. The Oxus, now known as the Amu Darya, rises in the Pamirs and flows for over fifteen hundred miles, carrying a huge volume of water from the

View of the Oxus emerging from the mountains into the steppe

snowy mountains of Central Asia. In ancient times the Oxus probably flowed into the Caspian, but geological conditions have radically changed since then. The level of the Caspian was eighty feet higher in Alexander's time. Today, the Amu Darya flows into the Aral Sea, east of the Caspian, a mighty stream whose waters have served to irrigate broad tracts of land from time immemorial. The Mongols destroyed the ancient and ingenious irrigation system but the Russians are currently doing their best to restore it.

Europeans seldom realize how closely their history is linked with that of Central Asia, although the mere mention of Huns, Mongols and Turks should be enough to remind us how often the steppe has affected our destiny. Like the Zagros, the Hindu Kush is a place of refuge whose valleys are inhabited by the survivors of many races which once played a major role in history. The Kafiri – a red-haired, blue-eyed people – still trace their descent from Alexander the Great's Greek settlers. Marco Polo, who visited them, confirmed this centuries ago. The Kafiri live in North-East Afghanistan, in a mountain belt bounded to the north by Russia, to the east by Tibet, and in the south by Pakistan. Their carvings, of which some examples can be seen in Kabul and others in Peshawar, are very remarkable. Although one cannot detect any classical Greek influence in them, they differ very markedly from all works of art found in neighbouring areas. The district was conquered by the Arabs and came under Islamic sovereignty, but it is noteworthy that, even in the Early Middle Ages, descent from Alexander's Greeks was still considered the supreme patent of nobility.

Wood-carvings produced by the Kafiri, who trace their descent from Alexander's Greek settlers

Bactria and Transoxiana contain few relics which can be directly associated with Alexander the Great himself. The massive earth rampart and walls of the acropolis at Balkh are still imposing, even in their ruined state, but it is doubtful whether Alexander actually installed his mobile headquarters inside this fortress. The ruins of ancient Bactra may lie buried beneath an insignificant mound a few miles to the east. Such mounds of rubble are very common in this part of Asia. Nobody knows what they conceal in many cases, but most of them are the remains of towns destroyed by the Mongols.

Bactra was the birthplace of Zoroaster, the founder of Iran's national religion. The city was well known in the West from the time of Alexander the Great onwards, and earned a reputation for wealth in Roman times. Bactra was the main entrepot for traders in Chinese silk. It was also the junction between the caravan route leading westwards to the Mediterranean and the track which led across the Hindu Kush, through the Kabul Valley, and over the Khyber Pass into India.

The ramparts of Balkh

Between the second century BC and the second century AD, the road that carried silk to the south also served to carry Buddhism from India, via Afghanistan, Transoxiana and the Tarim Basin, to China.

Alexander's first step on crossing the Oxus was to conquer the territory between that river and the Jaxartes. Now known as the Syr Darya, the Jaxartes starts life as a glacier stream in the rugged mountains of Tien-shan. From there it flows more than fifteen hundred miles through mountain and steppe to the Aral Sea, becoming a broad and powerful river on the way. The Jaxartes was the northern boundary of Alexander's conquests, and beyond it lay the broad domain of the Scythians.

Although the Greeks regarded the Scythians as barbarians, this does not mean that they were a people devoid of culture. Theirs was a nomadic culture, that was all. Arts and crafts took the place of architecture, and superb specimens of their handiwork are being unearthed in increasing numbers. We owe much of our knowledge of the Scythians to these articles which they abandoned for ever.

Mound near Balkh   *Source of the Jaxartes in the Tien-shan* ▶

Middle reaches of the Jaxartes ▶

Ornament on a gold comb. Scythian warriors in battle

Scythian artists were always responsive to external stimuli. Thus it is
that, according to their location within the migratory area, Scythian
works of art betray Chinese influence in the east, Iranian in the centre,
and Greek in the west. In turn, the Scythians' rich ornamentation
exerted an influence on races as remote as the Celts. The gold comb
from the Hermitage in Leningrad shows a horseman in combat with

Scythian vase, electrum. Warrior bandaging a wounded comrade

heavily armed foot-soldiers. This work of art dates from the fourth
century, that is to say, from Alexander's time. Another superb piece
in the Hermitage is the Scythian vase from Kul Oba illustrated above.
This shows one Scythian warrior bandaging another. Although a
product of nomadic culture it is not inferior in artistic merit to the
Greek vase already illustrated, which shows Achilles bandaging
Patroclus. The identity of theme is rather amusing.

Mud is the building material of the steppe, so most buildings of ancient date have disappeared. Apart from that, little digging has been done between the Oxus and Jaxartes. Near Samarkand, the Russians have recently excavated a city whose deepest layers antedate the Christian era. It may be that Alexander's original Marakanda will be discovered one day. Some archaeologists have identified a hill north of the city as the site of the acropolis where he held the feast which culminated in the murder of Cleitus.

The skill with which Greek artists portrayed human beings must have made a deep impression on the nomads of the steppe. Highly individualized plaster sculptures have been found in many places. The fierce warriors seem to have patronized Greek sculptors much as peasants used to cluster round the village photographer with requests for 'a good likeness'. This is how we come to possess the series of extremely lifelike heads which can now be seen in Kabul, Peshawar, and the Musée Guimet in Paris. Judging by his face, the grave, almost handsome warrior with the moustache may well be a Scythian. The man

Excavations at Samarkand

Plaster portrait of a Scythian ▶

*Portrait of a
helmeted warrior*

with the squat bossed helmet, an ugly but intelligent-looking individual, has Mongol features. Both portraits were produced by Greek artists, even though they date from a period when Greek kingdoms had ceased to exist in Central Asia. Many of the warriors against whom Alexander waged his guerilla campaign undoubtedly looked like this.

The Greek world which Alexander created in Asia showed a remarkable degree of vitality. The territories at the extreme limits of his empire originally formed part of the Seleucid possessions. In about 250 BC, however, Bactria asserted its independence under Diodotus I and the rulers of Bactria assumed royal prerogatives. In 208 BC they successfully foiled an attempt on the part of Antiochus the Great to compel Bactria to rejoin the Seleucid kingdom by force of arms. Greek Bactria retained its independence for a full generation longer than Alexander's native Macedonia. Perseus, the last king of Macedonia, was deposed by the Romans in 168 BC after the battle of Pydna, whereas eight years later Menander of Bactria was able to incorporate the whole of North-West India in his kingdom. In the north, Bactria's sovereignty at one stage extended as far as the Tarim Basin, at whose eastern oases Greek and Chinese merchants met to trade.

The Graeco-Bactrian kingdom fought with variable success against numerous enemies, among them the Scythians. We do not possess much in the way of detailed information about these conflicts. What we do have is a large number of coins minted by the kings of Bactria,

thydemus of Magnesia, who drove King Diodotus II from
throne and made himself king of Bactria and Sogdiana.
unified the country, repulsed an attack by the Seleucid
r Antiochus III, annexed two Parthian satrapies, and
quered parts of Chinese Turkestan. He died in 190 BC

Menander married Agathocleia, daughter of Demetrius, after
the latter's death. He ruled the bulk of Greek India until his
own death, which occurred between 150 and 145. Menander
is the only Greek to have gone down in Buddhist tradition as
a staunch defender of the faith

etrius, eldest son of Euthydemus, 190–167 BC, invaded
thern India in 184 and made Taxila his capital. He was
first ruler to strike coins bearing Greek and Indian
iptions. He was overthrown by Eucratides in 168 and
dered a year later

Eucratides, a prince of the Seleucid dynasty, invaded Bactria
in 168 BC and ascended the throne a year later. He was the
founder of the last Graeco-Bactrian dynasty, which continued
to rule until succeeded by the Kushan dynasty in 130 BC. His
son murdered him to succeed to the throne.

much prized by experts for their beauty and fine definition. Fortunately, the Bactrian kings were realistic and far-sighted men. Being as little vain as the barbarians of the steppe, they too insisted on a good likeness, with the result that we have some magnificent portraits of the principal rulers who, as heirs to Alexander the Great, made European history in the middle of Asia. The political skill with which the Greeks preserved their national independence for almost two hundred years – as long, in fact, as the Achaemenids had ruled – was remarkable enough. Even more remarkable was the way in which the spirit of Greece lived on after political autonomy had been lost.

One day in the early nineteen-thirties, French archaeologists working at Hadda unearthed a head which combined the attributes of Buddha and Apollo. It was extremely difficult to date the piece, but the current theory is that it originated in the third or fourth century AD. The Graeco-Bactrian kingdom had long disappeared from the political arena by that time. What was more, Iran and Mesopotamia were now ruled by the Parthians, so the Greeks of the East were isolated from the Hellenism of the Mediterranean area. Bactrian and Indian Greeks became Buddhists. It was centuries before Indian Buddhists took it into their heads to make effigies of Prince Gautama, the man who had attained nirvana, whereas the Greeks found it impossible to worship a god unless they could worship him in effigy.

All portrayals of the founder of Buddhism can be traced back to Greeks. Hadda, where archaeologists discovered the classically beautiful head illustrated opposite, was a Greek city in the east of Afghanistan. It is worth remembering that throughout the Oriental world, home of so many demonic deities, people have for two thousand years prayed to a Buddha whose effigy magically combines the mysticism of the Buddhist doctrine with the Apollonian lucidity of the Greeks.

Alexander set off for India with an army of a hundred thousand men, of whom no more than forty thousand can have been Macedonians. Settlers were required for the cities which he founded throughout the East. Luckily, the Greek motherland was rather overpopulated at this period, and colonial life has always had its attractions. None of Alexander's many foundations has yet been excavated, so we do not know whether they were genuine Greek *poleis* or simply Macedonian military posts. We are equally ignorant of how these places developed over the years. The Greek cities that have been excavated in Afghanistan and Pakistan are of later date.

Head of Buddha from Hadda, third–fourth century AD

The Khyber Pass. Caravan on the old camel-track. On the right, a modern road.

The Indus at Attock, near the confluence of the Kabul.
The army crossed the river not far upstream of this spot

The main body of the army, commanded by Hephaestion and Craterus, crossed the Khyber Pass and marched down to the Indus. After emerging from the Himalayas the Indus split up into a number of shallow and easily fordable streams, crocodiles being the only hazard. At Attock, now the site of a fortress built by the Mogul emperor Akbar, the river-valley narrowed again. Some way upstream but still in the plain, the Indus was joined by the Kabul. Alexander had given orders that the bridge which was to carry the army across the river should be sited to the north of this confluence.

Alexander himself had not followed the relatively convenient caravan route used in prehistoric times by the Indo-European invaders of Northern India. Instead, he struck farther north in order to pacify the mountain tribes which might have threatened his flank.

The Swat Valley in the Himalayas ▶

Archaeologists working in the valley of the Swat, a river running south-westwards from the Himalayas to the Kabul, have excavated the small town of Ora, now Udegram, which Alexander took after a brief siege. How the Macedonian army transported its siege-engines over these rugged mountain passes will always remain a mystery. The Swat Valley must have been the home of a particularly fine breed of cattle, because Alexander sent a herd back to Macedonia to improve the indigenous strain.

The citadel of Ora (left) and the small town of Ora
in the Swat Valley, captured by Alexander

Steep slope bordering the fortress of Aornos

After rejoining Hephaestion and Craterus, Alexander marched up the Indus again to capture Aornos. We are told that Aornos was a stronghold so spacious that sowing and reaping could be carried out within its defences. Steep slopes surrounded it on every side, and it was reputed to be capable of withstanding years of siege. Alexander took it at the first assault. The site of the fortress long eluded discovery and was only identified in recent times by Sir Aurel Stein, who traced it from a topographical description given by Arrian. It lies only a few miles north of the point where the Kabul flows into the Indus.

A longish halt was called at the Indus, during which time envoys arrived from the ruler of Taxila. This gave the army an opportunity to marvel at the wealth of an Indian maharajah. The prince presented Alexander with three thousand sacrificial beasts, ten thousand sheep, thirty war-elephants, and two hundred talents of silver – roughly £400,000. He also placed seven hundred well-armed cavalrymen at Alexander's disposal. In Taxila, the army became acquainted with one of the loveliest cities in contemporary India. Glittering festivals were held. All that the soldiers had heard about the wonders of India was surpassed by reality.

Resuming his eastward march, Alexander fought one more major

276

Alexander on horseback charging King Porus and his elephant

battle. Porus, a rival of Alexander's ally the rajah of Taxila, had drawn up his army beside the Hydaspes. The Indian king fought bravely, but Alexander managed to defeat him after a difficult river-crossing. The British Museum possesses two silver dekadrachms which were struck at Babylon to commemorate the battle. The one illustrated shows Alexander and Bucephalus charging King Porus, who is mounted on his war-elephant. Alexander not only allowed Porus to retain his possessions but added to them. He thereby created a balance of power between Porus and the ruler of Taxila which continued to serve its purpose until the former was murdered in 317, five years after Alexander's death.

During the march to the Hydaspes the army became acquainted with another of India's marvels – the tropical rainstorm. The Macedonians showed at the Hydaspes itself that long years of war had not impaired their courage – but what good is courage when every weapon rusts twice a day, every piece of leather goes mildewed, every item of equipment remains permanently damp, no tent can be pitched, and the whole unpleasant state of affairs lasts for weeks on end? It may be that what most contributed to ending the armed encroachment of West on East was the nightly rain in the jungles of the Punjab.

Although this book is not concerned with the centuries-long repercussions of Alexander's achievements, nor with the transformation of the world which his conquests brought about, attention must be drawn to at least one effect of the king's campaign. Alexander spent roughly two years in India, yet his brief sojourn there was still exerting a remarkable influence on the history of art five centuries later. The downfall of the Greek kingdom of Bactria did not spell the end of Greek culture in Central Asia and India. The period between the second and fourth centuries AD witnessed the development in the Kabul Valley–Hydaspes area of a thriving Indian art which was subject to Graeco-Roman influence. It is known, after the country which lay at the heart area of dissemination, as the art of Gandhara. Although certainly not to be compared with Greek art of the fourth century BC, it possesses great refinement. The delightful genie with the double-flute comes from Hadda, at the lower end of the Kabul Valley. The girl gracefully cupping a skull in her hands and the ecstatic demon in the fur robe date from the same period but may not have originated in the same atelier.

Sculptures from Hadda. Above left, a genie with a double-flute, and below, a girl with a human skull. Right, a demon

The genie with the flowers is reminiscent of the famous wax bust which Wilhelm von Bode acquired for Berlin as a work by Leonardo. The praying figure also comes from Hadda and probably belongs to the same period. Roman influence is clearly discernible in the sculptured frieze of Iranian warriors clad in the long trousers which formed part of their national costume.

Genie with flowers, from Hadda (left)
Praying figure from Hadda (right)
Warriors in Iranian costume. Relief

The aerial photographs of Charsadda, an archaeological site north
of Peshawar, shows a complete
Greek urban lay-out of the sort first
designed by the architect Hippo-
damus of Miletus for the city of
Rhodes in the fifth century BC. The
city of Charsadda is, of course,
older than the Greek city which
appears in our photograph. Known
as the lotus city, it was already renowned for its wealth and the
beauty of its architecture when
Darius the Great captured it in the
sixth century BC. Archaeologists
identified fifty-two separate layers.
The Taxila area contains a number of Greek cities built at quite widely
spaced intervals. The frieze illustrating a scene from Buddha's life was
found at Taxila itself. It is a very considerable aesthetic pleasure to see
a scene from the life of Buddha executed in the Graeco-Roman manner
and set in a Buddhist monastery whose columns have Attic bases and
composite Corinthian capitals. The gorgeous jewellery was once the
pride of an aristocratic lady from the wealthy city of Sirkap, one of
the later foundations in the vicinity of Taxila.

Frieze illustrating a scene from the life of Buddha

Jewellery of the Gandhara period from Sirkap-Taxila

283

Lower reaches of the Indus

The 'Voyage of a Thousand Ships' down the Indus did not pass without incident. Although the region had long resounded with tidings of Alexander's fame and everyone was convinced that he was in league with the gods and thus invincible, many of the small tribes inhabiting the banks of the great river fought bravely to preserve their independence. It was chiefly the Brahmans who, with a certain measure of fanaticism, kindled the rebellions which flared up all along the foreign invader's route. Being determined to make the Indus safe for commercial traffic, Alexander quelled the tribes one by one.

While storming the stronghold of the Malli the king was struck by an arrow. The wound was so serious that he almost died of its effects. Reduced to despair, the whole army lamented, prayed, and made sacrifice. The soldiers were convinced that their king's death would mean their own destruction. It is worth reflecting on the implications of this. Alexander's entourage included plenty of first-rate generals – Craterus was soon to lead the bulk of the army safely back to the West without the king's help – but only Alexander had the magic aura which made his army invincible.

The Indus Valley is the home of a very ancient civilization. Highly developed cities – the first in human history to be provided with drainage systems – existed there as early as the third millennium BC. The continuity of tradition is positively incredible. The carts driven by the peasants of Alexander's day – as of our own – were identical in construction with a toy of the Harappa culture unearthed at Mohenjo-Daro. The latter is at least three and a half thousand years old.

Model ox-cart from Mohenjo-Daro

Modern peasant ox-cart

As seamen, the Greeks of antiquity were surpassed only by the
Phoenicians. Their ship-building techniques were very advanced.
Vase-paintings show us what Greek ships of the fifth and fourth
centuries BC looked like. Nearchus' successful voyage from the Indus
Delta to the estuary of the Euphrates in the Persian Gulf says much
for the care lavished on its preparation. It should never be forgotten
that contemporary navigators were as ignorant of sextant and compass
as they were of the perils of the ocean. The phenomenon of tidal flow,
which the Greeks first encountered in the Indus Delta, was terrifying
enough in itself, so one can well imagine the superstitious dread which
seized the sailors when a school of whales surfaced not far from the
fleet. The Greeks were unaware of the very existence of such creatures.
Being an experienced commander, Nearchus summoned his trum-
peters and boosted morale by ordering them to blow a rousing fan-
fare. The sound of Greek trumpets was as awesome to the whales as
their own existence was to the Greeks. They dived and disappeared.
When the fleet and army once more came within sight of each other
in Carmania, something emerged which no one could have foreseen,
namely, that the army's march through Gedrosia had been a far more

Greek vase-paintings. Merchantmen and warships

dangerous undertaking than the fleet's voyage across the uncharted ocean.

Evidence of the care with which Alexander prepared his maritime expeditions can be seen in the Kuwait Museum on the Persian Gulf. Preserved there is a marble slab from Failaka, erected by a Greek sea-captain in gratitude to Zeus, Poseidon and Artemis for having saved him from shipwreck on the inhospitable shores of Arabia. It is probable that this sea-captain had been commissioned to gather information about sailing conditions for the benefit of Alexander's projected expedition from the Persian Gulf to the Red Sea.

Stone bearing a Greek inscription, unearthed on the island of Failaka in the Persian Gulf

The grim wilderness visible in our photograph of the Makran Desert
stretches for hundreds of miles. The army took two long months to
get clear of this comfortless waste. The success of the naval under-

View of the Makran Desert

taking was, in Alexander's own words, the greatest joy of his life. The king was not only a general and statesman but a promoter of scientific research.

Blind-man's buff

In Carmania, games were held to celebrate the happy reunion between army and fleet. This time, athletics were supplemented by the musical and dramatic contests which Alexander had forgone throughout his years in Bactria, Transoxiana and India. As we can see from vase-paintings, athletics had their lighter side. Although earlier than the fourth century, these vases are particularly fine, and the Olympic tradition was such that gymnastic exercises changed very little over long periods of time. Only the vase depicting youths dancing to the strains of a double-flute dates from Alexander's day. One can imagine how the rugged but rheumatic Macedonian veterans, who were just beginning to recuperate from their march through the desert, must have marvelled at the elegance of the young men's dancing. Attracted by Alexander's munificence, large numbers of artists flocked from every part of Hellas to compete in the artistic contests.

Athletes wrestling

Youths dancing to the music of a double-flute

Maenad dancing in the presence of Dionysus

290

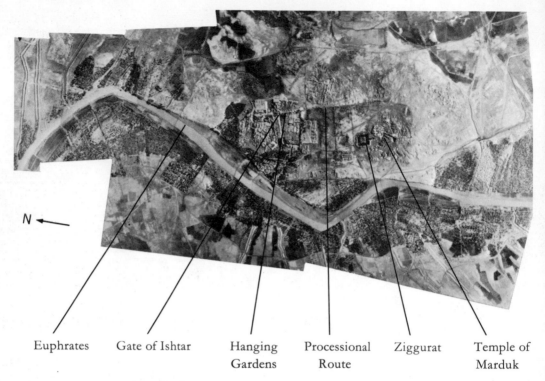

N ←

| Euphrates | Gate of Ishtar | Hanging Gardens | Processional Route | Ziggurat | Temple of Marduk |

Aerial view of Babylon   *Babylon. The Gate of Ishtar, built by Nebuchadnezzar II* ▶

Once more, and for the last time in its two thousand years of history, it fell to Babylon, the Gate of God, to become the capital of the world. Alexander designated the city his royal seat and gave orders that Hephaestion's body should be brought there from Ecbatana. The military tournament in honour of his friend's funeral was to be held at Babylon in the spring. Meanwhile, sinister omens began to multiply. Priests at the king's headquarters found numerous strange signs while studying the entrails of sacrificial beasts. The Chaldeans, long versed in the art of foretelling men's future from the stars, warned Alexander against moving to Babylon. However, none of these things could halt the march of destiny. Restlessly, the king tried to overcome his grief at the loss of Hephaestion, whose death had marked the end of his own youth, by immersing himself in new activities.

Envoys from all over the world came to pay their respects to Alexander during his months in Babylon. Those from Italy included Bruttians, Lucanians and Etruscans. We are not told whether the Romans did homage to him, but this is highly probable. Carthage also hailed the

293

The Sirrush, a mythical beast, from the Ishtar Gate

A bull from the Ishtar Gate. Tiled relief

new ruler of the East. Iberians from Spain and Celts from Gaul sent tokens of their amity and goodwill, as did the shrewd Ethiopians. The eyes of the entire world turned in fascination towards Babylon. Envoys were naturally instructed to probe Alexander's future plans, but none of the many projects under review ever came to fruition. Alexander died. His mind remained lucid to the last, despite his physical decline. For the last time, Alexander's veterans filed mutely past his couch. The only sign of recognition the king could still make was a slight movement of the hand.

Ptolemy had Alexander's body placed in a sumptuously decorated funeral carriage and escorted to Egypt by a splendid cortège. Ancient writers describe the hearse in such detail that it can be reconstructed with ease.

The king's last resting-place was Alexandria, where he was buried in a glass sarcophagus. It is not without deeper significance that the

The funeral carriage which conveyed Alexander the Great from Babylon to Egypt. Painting

Tomb of an unknown soldier belonging to the Macedonian army

transfer of Alexander's mortal remains was accompanied by a shift in the world's political centre of gravity. Shortly after Babylon had ceased to be the capital of Alexander's empire its long and glorious history came to an end. The city subsided into provincial insignificance and was eventually engulfed by drifting sand from the desert. Alexandria became the metropolis of the Mediterranean and remained so for a long time to come. Even when the last Macedonian occupant of the Egyptian throne died and Rome took possession of Alexandria, the only result was the conquest of Rome by Hellenism.

296

XIII   Alexander the Great with the body of Darius.
Persian miniature of the sixteenth century

Temple of the Alexander cult

Tomb of Cleopatra

Tomb of Alexander the Great

Roman lamp with a view of the tombs of Alexander the Great and Cleopatra on the discus

The Emperor Augustus paid homage to Alexander in his glass sarcophagus. An oil-lamp of the Roman period is embossed with a view of Alexandria, showing the tomb of Alexander the Great, the temple dedicated to his worship, and the tomb of Cleopatra. The tomb of an unknown soldier who belonged to the Macedonian army is preserved in a cemetery near Alexandria.

XIV Alexander the Great lying in state.
Persian–Mongol miniature of the fourteenth century

Mosque dedicated to the prophet Daniel at Alexandria, now demolished,
beneath which may lie the tomb of Alexander the Great

Alexander's own tomb, for so many hundreds of years the centre of
the Hellenistic world, has disappeared. Archaeological considerations
render it possible that it still exists beneath the mosque which the
Muslims erected in memory of the prophet Daniel after the Arab
conquest of Egypt.

Twelfth-century mosaic in Otranto Cathedral.
Alexander being carried skywards by two griffins

ALEXANDER THE GREAT, a man whose name had echoed round the world during his lifetime, lapsed into oblivion only a short time after he left the scene of his triumphs. The irony of this process lies in the fact that it occurred even though Alexander was eager for posthumous fame and went to considerable lengths to secure it. This aspect of his character could be construed as weakness, though as Dante himself says in Canto XXIV of the *Inferno*:

> 'For not on downy plumes, nor under shade
> Of canopy reposing fame is won;
> Without which whosoe'er consumes his days
> Leaveth such vestige of himself on earth
> As smoke in air or foam upon the wave.'

Even so, Pliny the Younger is obviously right when he insists that, far from being pursued, fame must follow us of its own accord. Alexander's very preoccupation with posthumous fame helped to engender a conspiracy of silence against his memory. At the same time, popular imagination seized upon the figure of this fantastic man and worked on it with such enthusiasm and perseverance that Alexander eventually became the national hero of almost every race conquered by him. Just to carry irony still further, the conspiracy of silence and the birth of the Alexander myth were associated with the same name. What occasioned the literary attack on Alexander the historical personage was the regrettable fate suffered at his headquarters by Callisthenes, Aristotle's nephew. The transformation of the authentic Alexander into a timeless myth first found expression in a literary work known as 'pseudo-Callisthenes'.

We have already discussed the reasons for the enduring tension which existed between Alexander and the Greeks. However greatly Alexander's political measures contributed to the future of Greece and however largely it was due to his genius that the achievements of classical Greece became the property of the whole world, the Greeks persisted in regarding Chaeronea as the battle which lost them their freedom. Again, however deleterious the effects of their appalling particularism in politics and of the grim and perpetual civil wars between city and city, at least it was their own freedom which the Greeks were abusing. To the modern European, Alexander's preservation of the cultural heritage of Greece was his crowning achievement. Little importance is attached to the price which the Greeks had to pay as a result. One wonders what our own reaction would be if we were confronted by the prospect of saving the cultural heritage of Europe at the expense of our personal freedom.

At the turn of the century, venerable professors still regarded Demosthenes as the great man, not Alexander. The brilliant historian George Grote concluded his twelve-volume work on the history of Greece, written between 1846 and 1856, with a passage which can only be likened to an obituary notice:

'I have now outlined the history of Greece down to the end of Alexander's generation, the period which not only witnessed the annihilation of Greek political freedom and independence but also coincided with the incipient flagging of creative genius and the decline of that consummate scientific and rhetorical greatness and glory which emerged in Plato and Demosthenes during the fourth century. The contents of the latter part of the present volume reveal only too clearly that Greece had ceased to exist as a specific historical entity. We have described Alexander and his conquests – a non-Greek conqueror in whose vast possessions the Greeks became lost, their intellectual brilliance dimmed, their spirit broken, their manhood half shorn by Zeus: melancholy and enervated victims overtaken by the day of servitude.'

Grote did not recognize Hellenism as a concept. The picture changes when we come to his contemporary Droysen, who wrote the first coherent account of the Hellenistic period, but the most intelligent assessment of Alexander and his achievements can be found in Jacob Burckhardt.

Nevertheless, even if there were some distinguished scholars of a century ago who still regarded freedom as irrevocable, one cannot blame the Greeks in whose lifetime that freedom was lost for having opposed both Philip II and Alexander. There were other reasons for the conspiracy of silence.

Alexander's existence transformed not only the world but also the methods used to describe it. The Hellenistic period introduced a new form of historical representation. Where this change in historical method is concerned, right is demonstrably on the side of those authorities who believe that the new age which dawned with Alexander had long been in preparation. Hadas illustrates this in his excellent book *Kultur des Hellenismus*. All the historians of the fourth century were pupils of Isocrates, the man who had begged King Philip to take Hellas under his protection. Isocrates had no time for the sort of freedom which no one knows how to employ properly. Unfortunately for us, quotations in ancient writers are all that survive of the work of his leading pupil, Theopompus of Chios, even though he was widely read as late as the Byzantine period. Although Theopompus' *Hellenica* only covered the reign of Philip II, his breadth of vision is already tinged with the universalism which Alexander converted into the cosmopolitan spirit of Hellenism. Just as Alexander made the transition to international politics, so historians began to write on a universal scale.

Alexander, who bemoaned the fact that no Homer would ever sing his praises, found no historian of the first rank among the scholars of his time. Several of the men who took part in his campaign wrote historical works. Foremost among these works were a biography of Alexander written by Ptolemy when he became king of Egypt and an account by Nearchus, who commanded the naval expedition from the Indus to the Euphrates. No contemporary account has survived, but decades of the most laborious and minute philological study have enabled scholars to tell which passages in biographies of the Roman period were taken from earlier works. The man chosen by Alexander to pay literary tribute to his achievements was Callisthenes, who had been recommended for the post of official court historian by Aristotle himself. No student of history could have been presented with a grander task. Able to observe the course of Alexander's campaign at first hand, granted free access to the Ephemerides or daily entries in the war-diary kept at headquarters, and frequently invited to dine with a king who respected scholarship, Callisthenes had every opportunity to become an Alexander among historians. Although a man of great erudition, he failed. Callisthenes worked with Aristotle for many years and had known Alexander at home in Pella. He conducted a lively correspondence with Aristotle and kept him informed of the natural phenomena which he encountered in such profusion in remote and unfamiliar lands. He continued to participate in the campaign until his death. All in all, he was well qualified to fulfil his role as chronicler to Alexander the Great. The failings on which he foundered were inherent in his character. He combined the contempt felt by Greek for Macedonian with the disdain felt by a scholar for military men, nor did he trouble to conceal his feelings from those whose undeniable merits had earned them a high place in the king's esteem. Needless to say, these exalted individuals paid him back in the same coin. He was positively loathed at headquarters and did not get on well with the king either. Even in the presence of Alexander, himself a Macedonian, Callisthenes did not disguise his contempt for his surroundings. On the other hand, surviving fragments of his work show that he was not above injecting exaggerated flattery into his account of the king's career. Alexander set little store by this. Lucian reports that, while reading one of these fulsome passages as he sailed down the Indus, the king tossed the manuscript overboard and observed caustically that the author ought to be thrown in after it. Callisthenes took his cue from Aristotle in rejecting Alexander's grand vision of an *oecumene* embracing East and West. It will always be a source of wonder that Aristotle, who did so much for the future of the West, persisted so stubbornly in regarding non-Greeks as human beings of inferior status.

Unable to cope with the hostile intrigues engendered by his own stupidity, Callisthenes blundered into the treason trial which put paid to his career. It is not clear from written sources whether or not he was really guilty, and it is equally uncertain whether he was actually executed.

Callisthenes belonged to the Peripatetic school. His fellow-academics unanimously branded the sentence passed on him and confirmed by Alexander as murder. In consequence, philosophers embarked on a spiteful campaign against the memory of the great king after his death. At the same time, myth started to run riot. Since the Peripatetics continued to play a dominant role in Hellenistic intellectual life for many generations, Alexander receded more and more into the background of historical writing as time went by – so much so that the literature of the second century BC is devoid of references to his name.

The effects of Alexander's unpopularity with Hellenic literati endured for a long time to come. The Roman philosopher Seneca took the opportunity, when quoting Callisthenes, to vent his own spleen on

*XV   Aristotle teaching Alexander as a boy. French miniature from
'Le livre et la vraye hystoire du bon roy Alixandre'*

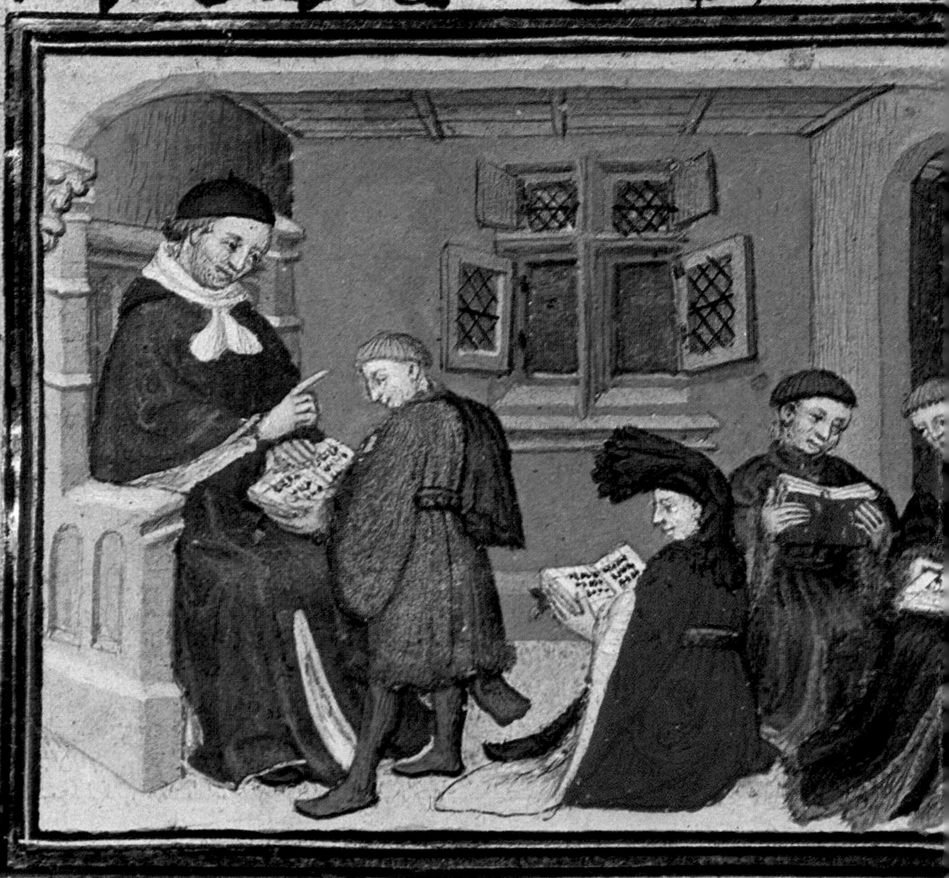

pez quant il
fu saure le roy
phe le fist mett
a leseolle aropai
que senfans de gentilz homes
Lequel Alixandre en liue et
en paroles les surmotoit tout
et aussi faisoit il degtes sem
blabes en vigueur Dont il
aduint que auant que il

the 'raging' king and his 'eternal crime'. In turn, Petrarch quotes this passage from Seneca in his *Life of Alexander*. Finally, the philosopher's aversion to Alexander can still be detected in our own era.

Ironically enough, the ancient writer who eventually broke the evil spell that had been cast on Alexander was another Greek, Plutarch of Chaeronea. Plutarch, who had in his boyhood played beside the marble lion commemorating the battle of Chaeronea, inaugurated the literary career which was to earn him such renown with a brilliant and eminently readable defence of Alexander the Great.

The *Anabasis Alexandri* by Flavius Arrianus proved to be crucial to the king's reputation. This excellent work, on which our existing knowledge of Alexander's achievements largely depends, originated in auspicious circumstances. Arrian was born at the end of the first century AD at Nicomedia in Bithynia. For a man destined to write a history of Alexander, this was a distinct advantage. Nicomedia was situated beside the Sea of Marmora in an area whose continuous political tensions gave Arrian a thorough insight into the problems of the East at an early age. He acquired the military knowledge essential to an expert assessment of Alexander's feats of generalship during a brilliant career as an officer in Emperor Hadrian's army. On his retirement, the Emperor appointed him governor of the East Anatolian province of Cappadocia, where he became acquainted with the problems of government in an oriental country. Being a place where Hellenic and Iranian influences met and mingled, Cappadocia had early played an important role in the evolution of Hellenism. Thus, Arrian actually lived in a world of which Alexander had only dreamed. The third fortunate circumstance was that Arrian still had access to the ancient literature on Alexander which has since been lost. The product of these happy coincidences was a historical work whose subject matter alone was enough to invest it with importance.

About a century after Arrian's death there appeared at Alexandria a fanciful work on Alexander which was originally published under Callisthenes' name. Since we know that the book was spurious and quite unconnected with Callisthenes, it is referred to as 'pseudo-Callisthenes'. It was, in fact, the first edition of the *Romance of Alexander*. The *Romance* has been translated into thirty languages, even including Icelandic. It was continually added to, amended, expanded and re-published until the Middle Ages, thus becoming one of the world's most widely read books.

The *Romance of Alexander* is a splendid compound of fact and fantasy. The first edition contained some letters to and from Alexander. They were forged, though with an intelligence surpassed only by the intelligence of those who detected the forgeries. In the course of time, the manuscript became infiltrated by legends that had sprung from the popular imagination, and fact and fiction were mingled with free artistic licence. On the one hand there is Alexander's conversation with Indian sages, which actually took place; on the other, his conversation with Queen Candace of Meroe in the Sudan, who lived three centuries after his time. The *Romance* relates how Alexander undertook a journey to the land of eternal night in quest of the water of life. He also went on an air-trip by courtesy of two griffins, who transported him through the sky. Representations of this latter incident are scattered half-way across the globe. They can be found in ancient Ethiopic manuscripts, in a twelfth-century mosaic in Otranto Cathedral (p. 299), in a Romanesque frieze in the cathedral at Freiburg im Breisgau, and on a capital in Basle Cathedral. The scene is, however, far from religious in tone. With charming naivety, the griffins are always shown snapping greedily at some sort of bait above their heads as they flutter skywards with Alexander, who is sometimes shown seated in a cage. Alexander's journey into the sky was later matched by a journey to the bed of the ocean. The Egyptian version of the *Romance* embodies the myth that Alexander's father was Nectanebo, the last of the Pharaohs, who consorted with Olympias in the guise of Zeus Ammon. Editions of the *Romance* varied in text according to the language in which they were published. In the Persian version, Alexander was the offspring of a union between the Persian king Ochus (Artaxerxes III) and a daughter of King Philip II of Macedonia. He conquered not only the whole of India but Tibet and China as well. It is understandable, therefore, that although the Persians still think of the historical Alexander as a barbarian who set fire to Persepolis, the legendary Alexander continued to figure in Persian art even in the Middle Ages. The *Iskandernama*, an epic work on the Alexander theme by the famous twelfth-century poet Nizami, consists of ten thousand lines. One miniature from a sixteenth-century version of the work shows Alexander kneeling on the ground with Darius' lifeless head in his lap (Colour Plate XIII). A fourteenth-century miniature of the Ilkhan period from the *Shahnama*, Firdousi's 'Book of Kings', shows Alexander being placed in his funeral carriage (Colour Plate XIV). The scene is depicted in great detail. Four tall candles stand at the corners of the hearse, and above and to the side hang glass lamps of the type commonly found in mosques. Aristotle is standing behind the coffin and Olympias has flung herself on it in a transport of grief.

In the Jewish tradition, Alexander becomes the 'Master of the Throne of Solomon'. He has two horns, and the high priest proclaims him to be the ruler of the fourth kingdom of the world prophesied by Daniel. Here, Alexander passes for a precursor of the Messiah.

Christian monks characterized Alexander as a saintly ascetic. Islam not only regarded him as the Two-Horned One, like the Jews, but turned him into a prophet as well, the *Koran* calls him Dhulkarnein, and he features in Arab legends as Iskander, a name much favoured by Muslims to this day. When Napoleon landed in Egypt the Bedouins believed that the King of Macedonia had returned.

In medieval France, Alexander became a knight. A fifteenth-century miniature from the 'vraye hystoire du bon roy Alixandre' (Colour Plate XV) shows a youthful Alexander being taught by Aristotle. *The Battle of Arbela* (Gaugamela), a sixteenth-century painting by Albrecht Altdorfer of Regensburg, which is now in the Alte Pinakothek in Munich, is one of the major examples of German art. Colour Plate XVI reproduces a detail of this picture. Alexander's remarkable personality may justly be said to have exercised the imagination of the entire world.

The first honorific epithet appended to Alexander's name was Aniketos, 'the Invincible', a title which he bore during his lifetime. Alexander carefully nurtured his reputation for invincibility – in fact, there were quite a few military operations which he might just as well have avoided if he had not wished to preserve that reputation. His second epithet, 'the Great', was bestowed on him by the Romans a few decades after his death, who rendered him this honour with ungrudging magnanimity. Despite this, old Appius Claudius, the builder of the celebrated Appian Way, saw fit when opposing a peace offer from King Pyrrhus of Epirus in the Senate to insist that if Alexander had been obliged to fight the Romans he might have remained great but ceased to be invincible.

Alexander was the first ruler in world history to be called 'the Great', though two earlier monarchs – the Persian kings Cyrus I and Darius I – received the same accolade at a later date. According to Pfister, posterity has bestowed the title on some fifty historical figures only. Anyone wishing to learn something about the magic of fame would be well advised to take a closer look at this illustrious gathering.

The next man to be called 'great' by the Romans was Hanno, the Carthaginian general who fought against them in the Punic Wars not long afterwards. He was followed by the Parthian king Mithridates II, who died in 88 BC, and his opponent Pompey. Unfamiliar as it sounds to our ears, the Romans also christened Caesar 'the Great'. The Emperor Alexander Severus was a notable exception, when the Senate offered him the title 'Magnus' he displayed true greatness by declining it.

There is subtle humour in the anecdote which tells how Hannibal expressed himself on the subject of historical greatness. One day in Ephesus, after his flight from Carthage, Hannibal encountered Scipio the Elder, the man who had defeated him at Zama. Scipio asked the Carthaginian victor of Cannae whom he considered to be the three greatest generals in history. Hannibal listed Alexander, Pyrrhus, and himself. Scipio laughed and asked him what his answer would have been if he, Hannibal, had defeated him, Scipio. 'Ah,' Hannibal replied lightly, 'I would then come before Alexander.'

Caesar is followed by a truly remarkable gallery of 'greats' including the emperors Constantine I and Theodosius I, and, finally, during the transition to the Middle Ages, Charlemagne, King of the Franks and Roman Emperor.

Many of the 'greats' – e.g. Alphonso III of Castille, Prince Stephen III of Rumania and King Manoel I of Portugal – would tax even an expert knowledge of history. Also known as 'the Great' are the Turkish sultan Suleiman II, the Mongol emperor Akbar, and Shah Abbas I of Persia. The title never caught on in the case of Louis XIV, but his contemporary in Brandenburg became known as the Great Elector. Only three women in history have been accorded nominal greatness – a nun, a noblewoman, and an empress. The first was Gertrude of Helfta, the second Matilda, Margravine of Tuscany, a friend of Pope Gregory VII, and the third Empress Catherine of Russia. Entwined round the concept of historical greatness like a fine arabesque is the fact that one scholar has also gone down in history as 'great', namely, Albertus Magnus, the teacher of Thomas Aquinas.

Philosophers have always liked to ponder on the great ones of this world, but the magic of fame is unfathomable. We cannot tell what standards are applied to human achievement by Clio, the Muse of History, when she bestows her supreme title. We only know that there lies concealed in her name the Greek word

ΚΛΕΟΣ, – FAME

LIST AND SOURCES OF ILLUSTRATIONS

94 Persepolis. The Great Staircase leading to the terrace, late sixth century BC. Photo Roloff Beny

95 Persepolis. The Gate of Xerxes, fifth century BC. Photo Dietrich Berndt

96 Persepolis. The Apadana or audience-chamber with the east stairway in the background, sixth–fifth century BC. Photo Dietrich Berndt
Persepolis. Gold foundation tablet in original stone case, unearthed in the Apadana, late sixth century BC. Photo Georges Bourdelon

97 Persepolis. Griffin-headed capital, fifth–fourth century BC. Photo Dietrich Berndt

98–99 Persepolis. Frieze of bodyguards on the north side of the east stairway to the Apadana, sixth–fifth century BC. Photo Roloff Beny

100 Persepolis. Detail from the relief beside the east stairway to the Apadana. Syrians or Lydians with amphorae, bowls and arm-bands, sixth–fifth century BC. Photo Antonello Perissinotto

101 Gold bowl engraved with the name of King Xerxes, fifth century BC, probably from Hamadan. Museum of Archaeology, Teheran. Photo Josephine Powell
Gold arm-band from the Oxus Treasure, sixth–fourth centuries BC. British Museum, London. Photo courtesy of the Trustees of the British Museum
Silver amphora with handles in the form of horses, fifth–fourth century BC. Private collection, Basle. Photo L'Univers des Formes—Draeger Frères

102 Handle of an amphora in the form of a winged ibex, found in Armenia. Silver, partly gilded, c. 380 BC. Staatliche Museen, Berlin. Photo courtesy of the museum

103 Gold figurine of a Bactrian camel, probably from Hamadan, fifth–fourth century BC. Private collection, New York. Photo Musée Cernuschi, Paris
Gold ear-rings, fifth–fourth centuries BC. Left: Musée du Louvre, Paris. Photo Archives Photographiques. Centre: Musée du Louvre, Paris. Photo courtesy of the museum. Right: Private collection, Teheran. Photo Dr A. Razavi

104–105 Persepolis. Palace of Darius the Great, sixth–fifth centuries BC. Photo Dietrich Berndt

106 Persepolis. Relief on the east gate of the tripylon. Darius the Great and Xerxes, sixth–fifth centuries BC. Photo courtesy of the Oriental Institute, University of Chicago

107 Darius the Great on his throne. Detail from a painted amphora from Canosa, fourth century BC. Museo Nazionale, Naples. Photo Soprintendenza alle Antichità della Campania, Naples

108–109 View from the terrace at sunset. Photo James Burke, Life Magazine © 1967, Time Inc.
Persepolis. Relief of a serving-woman on a doorpost in the palace of Darius the Great, sixth–fifth centuries BC. Photo Dietrich Berndt

110–111 Naksh-i-Rustam. Rock face housing the tombs of the Achaemenid kings. Photo courtesy of the Oriental Institute, University of Chicago

112 Naksh-i-Rustam. Tomb of Darius the Great, d. 485 BC. Photo Dietrich Berndt

113 Naksh-i-Rustam. Sassanian rock sculpture: King Shapur I triumphing over the Roman emperors Philip the Arab and Valerian, second half of third century AD. Photo Dietrich Berndt

114 Naksh-i-Rustam. Sassanian rock sculpture: investiture of King Ardashir I by Ahuramazda, third century AD. On the right, remains of an Elamite cult relief of the second millennium BC. Photo Roloff Beny

III THE SPLENDID BEGINNING

115 Greek and Persian in hand-to-hand combat. Detail from the Alexander Sarcophagus commissioned by King Abdalonymus of Sidon, late fourth century BC. Museum of Archaeology, Istanbul. Photo Dieter Johannes

122–123 Bird's-eye impression of the Dardanelles and Hellespont. Copperplate engraving from G. J. Grelot: Relation d'un Voyage de Constantinople, 1680: 1689 edition

125 Northern slopes of Hissarlik, the hill that once was Troy. Photo Cincinnati Archaeological Expedition

126 View of the Scamandrian Plain from Troy. In the background, the Gallipoli Peninsula. Photo Roloff Beny

127 Obverse of a silver tetrobol bearing the portrait of Spithridates, governor of Lydia and Ionia, c. 334 BC. British Museum, London. Photo Peter Clayton
The Granicus, where Alexander the Great first defeated the Persians in 334 BC. Photo W. Leaf, courtesy of the Royal Geographical Society, London

128 Dascylium, now Eregli. Fragment of a Graeco-Persian relief of a mounted procession, fifth century BC. Museum of Archaeology, Istanbul. Photo courtesy of the museum

129 Dascylium, now Eregli. Fragment of a Graeco-Persian relief of a sacrificial rite, fifth century BC. Museum of Archaeology, Istanbul. Photo courtesy of the museum

130–131 Sardis. Temple of Artemis-Cybele, third century BC. Photo Hirmer Fotoarchiv, Munich

133 King Croesus on his pyre. Amphora attributed to Myson, possibly from Vulci, c. 500 BC. Musée du Louvre, Paris. Photo Hirmer Fotoarchiv, Munich

134–135 Ephesus. Remains of the Artemision with Seljuk mosque and Ottoman castle in the background. Photo courtesy of General Sir James Marshall-Cornwall

176 Oasis of Siwa. Temple of Zeus Ammon. Photo Captain R. Briggs, courtesy of the Royal Geographical Society, London

IV VICTORY WITHOUT END

177 Bilingual Graeco-Aramaic inscription of King Asoka, 259–226 BC, found near Kandahar. On permanent loan to the Museo Nazionale d'Arte Orientale, Rome. Excavated by the Italian Archaeological Mission in Afghanistan. Photo G. Silvestrini (Gabinetto Fotografico Nazionale, Rome)

184 Upper reaches of the Euphrates near Elazig in Eastern Turkey. Photo J. J. H. Clowes

186–187 Lower reaches of the Euphrates (Shatt el-Arab). Photo Editions Arthaud (M. Audrain)

188 Middle reaches of the Euphrates. Photo André Parrot

189 Gold model of a Persian chariot from the Oxus Treasure, sixth–fourth centuries BC. British Museum, London. Photo courtesy of the Trustees of the British Museum

190 Persepolis. Detail from a procession of tribute-bearers on the east stairway of the Apadana, sixth–fifth centuries BC. Photo courtesy of the Oriental Institute, University of Chicago
Greek hoplite in combat with a Persian cavalry-man. Seal impression, fifth–fourth centuries BC. Private collection. From H. Seyrig: 'Cachets Achéménides' in *Archaeologica Orientalia in Memoriam Ernst Herzfeld*, New York 1952, Plate XXXI, I
Bronze statuette of an Iranian horseman, sixth–fourth centuries BC. British Museum, London. Photo courtesy of the Trustees of the British Museum

191 Funerary gift in the form of a horse. Chinese ceramic of the T'ang dynasty. Ashmolean Museum, Oxford. Photo courtesy of the museum

193 Europe and Asia supporting a plaque commemorating the battle of Gaugamela above an altar. Drawing based on a Roman relief, first century AD. Palazzo Chigi, Rome. From Otto Jahn: *Griechische Bilderchroniken*, Bonn 1873, Plate VI, M

194–195 Babylon. Baroque reconstruction. Copper-plate engraving from Johannes Bernhard Fischer von Erlach: *Entwurff einer historischen Architectur*, 1721

198 Relief from Messene, possibly of Alexander and Craterus lion-hunting, fourth century BC. Musée du Louvre, Paris. Photo Giraudon

199 Drawing of a carnelian intaglio showing Alexander being rescued from a lion by Craterus. Hellenistic, formerly in the collection of Sir Arthur Evans. From Paul Perdrizet: 'Venatio Alexandri' in *Journal of Hellenic Studies*, XIX, (1899), Plate XI, 3

Cast of a pottery mould from Arezzo. Alexander and Craterus hunting lion, between 25 BC and AD 25. British Museum, London. Photo courtesy of the Trustees of the British Museum

200 Susa. The so-called tomb of the prophet Daniel. Photo A. Costa

202–203 Susa. Aerial photo courtesy of the Oriental Institute, University of Chicago

204 Susa. Pottery beaker with geometrical design, c. 3500 BC. British Museum, London. Photo Edwin Smith

Susa. Bronze model representing a religious ceremony, twelfth century BC. Musée du Louvre, Paris. Photo Archives Photographiques

205 Susa. Relief on the head of the basalt stele bearing the laws of Hammurabi: the king conversing with the god Shamash, c. 1930–1888 BC. Musée du Louvre, Paris. Photo Hirmer Fotoarchiv, Munich

Susa. Detail from the Hammurabi stele showing cuneiform inscription, c. 1930–1888 BC. Musée du Louvre, Paris. Photo Hirmer Fotoarchiv, Munich

206 Susa. Bull capital belonging to one of the columns which supported the roof of the Apadana, late sixth century BC. Musée du Louvre, Paris. Photo Archives Photographiques

207 Susa. Winged and horned lion. Glazed tiles from the Palace of Darius, sixth century BC. Musée du Louvre, Paris. Photo M. Chuzeville

208 Plinth of the monument to the tyrannicides Harmodius and Aristogeiton, found in the Athenian Agora, 477–476 BC. Photo Agora Excavations, American School of Classical Studies, Athens

209 Harmodius and Aristogeiton. Roman copies based on originals of the late fifth century BC. Museo Nazionale, Naples. Photo Mansell-Alinari

210–211 Persepolis. Relief from the treasury: Darius the Great granting an audience, sixth–fifth century BC. Museum of Archaeology, Teheran. Photo courtesy of Oriental Institute, University of Chicago

212 Sarnath. Capital of King Asoka's column, 242–236 BC. Sarnath Museum. Photo Dr Martin Hürlimann

213 Persepolis. Bronze stand in the form of three lions, sixth–fifth century BC. Museum of Archaeology, Teheran. Photo Publications Filmée d'Art et d'Histoire, Paris

Persepolis. Base of a column beside the Gate of Xerxes, fifth century BC. Photo Lucien Hervé

214–215 Boy driving donkeys along a valley in the Zagros Mountains. Photo Dietrich Berndt

216 Camel train near Tabas. Photo A. Costa

217 Nomads' tents in the mountains. Photo Paul Popper

269 Hadda. Buddha, plaster, third–fourth centuries AD. Kabul Museum. Photo Josephine Powell

270 Camel train in the Khyber Pass. Photo Paul Popper

271 Attock. Fortress guarding the Indus Valley, built by the Mogul emperor Akbar in 1581. Photo Josephine Powell

272–273 The Swat Valley. View from the village of Bahrein. Photo Roger Wood

274 Ora (Udegram). View of the citadel excavated by the Italian Archaeological Mission in Swat. Photo F. Bonardi

275 Ora (Udegram). View of the site excavated by the Italian Archaeological Mission in Swat. Photo F. Bonardi

276 Aornos (Pir Sar), besieged by Alexander in 326 BC. Photo Sir Aurel Stein, courtesy of the Royal Geographical Society, London

277 Obverse of a silver decadrachm struck at Babylon to celebrate Alexander's defeat of King Porus (326 BC). British Museum, London. Photo John Webb

278 Hadda. Plaster relief of a genie playing a double-flute, third–fourth centuries AD. Musée Guimet, Paris. Photo Editions des Musée Nationaux

Hadda. Plaster relief of a girl holding a skull, third–fourth centuries AD. Musée Guimet, Paris. Photo Editions des Musées Nationaux

279 Hadda. Plaster relief of a demon in an animal skin, third–fourth centuries AD. Musée Guimet, Paris. From J.-J. Barthoux: *Fouilles de Hadda*, Plate 45

280 Hadda. Plaster statuette of a genie with flowers, third–fourth centuries AD. Musée Guimet, Paris. Photo Editions des Musées Nationaux

281 Hadda. Plaster relief of a praying figure, third–fourth centuries AD. Musée Guimet, Paris. Photo Editions des Musées Nationaux

Gandhara. Stone frieze of figures in Iranian costume, second–third centuries AD. Museum of Archaeology, Toronto. From *Syria*, 1960. Plate X, 6

282 Charsadda. Aerial view of Shaikhan Dheri, showing part of an urban complex dating from the second century BC. Photo Pakistan Air Force

Taxila. Relief illustrating a scene from the life of Buddha, second–third centuries AD. National Museum of Pakistan, Karachi. Photo courtesy of the museum

283 Taxila. Graeco-Roman jewellery from Sirkap, first century BC/AD. National Museum of Pakistan, Karachi. Photo Frances Mortimer

284 The Indus near Sukkur. Photo Josephine Powell

285 Mohenjo-Daro. Clay model of an ox-cart, 2500–1500 BC. National Museum of Pakistan, Karachi. From Sir John Marshall: *Mohenjo-Daro*, Plate CLIV, 10

Mohenjo-Daro. Modern ox-cart. Photo Frances Mortimer

286 Attic kylix depicting a Greek merchantman and a warship, c. 540 BC. British Museum, London. Photo courtesy of the Trustees of the British Museum

287 Bowl signed by Nicosthenes, depicting two Greek ships under sail, c. 520 BC. Musée du Louvre, Paris. Photo Hirmer Fotoarchiv, Munich

Failaka in the Persian Gulf. Stone bearing inscription dedicated by Soteles to Zeus, Poseidon and Artemis, probably fourth century BC. Kuwait Museum. Drawn by Margaret Thomas

288–289 View of the Makran Desert. Photo Sir Aurel Stein, courtesy of the Royal Geographical Society, London

290 Youths playing ephedrismos. Oenochoe by the Shuvalov Painter, c. 425 BC. Staatliche Museen, Berlin. Photo Hirmer Fotoarchiv, Munich

Wrestlers. Amphora by the Andocides Painter, c. 530–520 BC. Staatliche Museen, Berlin. Photo Hirmer Fotoarchiv, Munich

291 Two youths dancing to a double-flute. Boeotian basin from the Cabiri shrine near Thebes, fourth century BC. Staatliche Museen, Berlin. Photo courtesy of the museum

Maenads playing the double-flute and dancing to Dionysus. Volute crater by the Carneia Painter, c. 410 BC. Museo Nazionale Archeologico, Taranto. Photo Hirmer Fotoarchiv, Munich

292 Babylon. Aerial photograph courtesy of the Director-General of Antiquities, Baghdad

293 Babylon. The Ishtar Gate, seventh–sixth centuries BC. Photograph courtesy of the Director-General of Antiquities, Baghdad

294 Babylon. Drawing of a *sirrush* from the Ishtar Gate, seventh–sixth centuries BC. From *Mitteilungen der Deutschen Orientgesellschaft*, 1902

Babylon. Drawing of a bull from the Ishtar Gate, seventh–sixth centuries BC. From *Mitteilungen der Deutschen Orientgesellschaft*, 1902

295 Alexander's funeral procession. Painting by André Bauchant, 1940. Tate Gallery, London. Photograph courtesy Trustees of the Tate Gallery

296 Alexandria. Macedonian cavalry officer on a painted tombstone from the Sciatbi necropolis, late fourth century BC. Musée Gréco-Romain, Alexandria. From Evaristo Breccia: *La Necropoli di Sciatbi*, 1912, Plate XXII

297 Alexandria. Roman lamp bearing a representation of the harbour and the royal necropolis, first century AD. Hermitage, Leningrad. Photo courtesy of the museum

298 Alexandria. The Nebi Daniel Mosque, possibly built on the site of Alexander's tomb. Photo Viollet

EPILOGUE: THE MAGIC OF FAME

299 Alexander transported into the sky by two
griffins. Mosaic pavement by Pantaleon in
Otranto Cathedral, 1163–1166. Photo Mansell-
Alinari

COLOUR PLATES

316

GAUGAMELA
Hard-won victory over the second Persian army. Darius flees to High Iran

The Caspian Gates

DAMGHAN
Darius is abandoned by his remaining supporters and found dying by a Macedonian soldier

ECBATANA
New base for the eastern campaign, commanded by Parmenion, later murdered here

Euphrates

Tigris

SUSA

BABYLON

323 B C

Order restored and preparations made for an expedition to Arabia, the Red Sea and Ethiopia. Alexander succumbs to an attack of fever

330 B C

324 B C

PERSEPOLIS Vast quar seized and burned de

The Persian Gates